YOU TOO CAN LIVE THE DREAM

10 STEPS TO ACHIEVING THE AMERICAN DREAM

Dixion Rwakasyaguri

DEiL BOOKS
FREDERICK, MARYLAND

Copyright © 2018 by Dixion Rwakasyaguri.

All rights reserved. No part of this publication may be reproduced, distributed or transmitted in any form or by any means, including photocopying, recording, or other electronic or mechanical methods, without the prior written permission of the publisher, except in the case of brief quotations embodied in critical reviews and certain other noncommercial uses permitted by copyright law. For permission requests, write to the publisher, addressed "Attention: Permissions Coordinator," at the address below.

Dixion Rwakasyaguri/DEiL BOOKS
P.O.Box 1350
Frederick, MD 21702-0350
https://www.deilbooks.com

Publisher's Note: While the author has taken utmost efforts to ensure the accuracy of the written content, all readers are advised to follow information mentioned herein at their own risk. The author cannot be held responsible for any personal or commercial damage caused by misinterpretation of information. All readers are encouraged to seek professional advice when needed.

Ordering Information:
Quantity sales. Special discounts are available on quantity purchases by corporations, associations, and others. For details, contact the "Special Sales Department" at the address above.

You Too Can Live The Dream/ Dixion Rwakasyaguri. -- 1st ed.
ISBN 978-0-9986251-0-2

Contents

INTRODUCTION 1

Integrating into a New Culture While Maintaining Your Roots 13

Avoiding Pitfalls and Overcoming Challenges 27

Obtaining a Solid Education and Acquiring Financial Literacy.. 41

Identifying Your Path and Securing the Right Job 53

Building and Preserving Fruitful Relationships 61

Purchasing a Home 75

Establishing and Running a Successful Business........... 87

Enlisting and Serving in the US. Military 99

Reaping Rewards and Giving Back 111

Living the Dream 119

A WORD OF THANKS.. 129

I dedicate this book ...

To my beautiful wife, my lovely flower -Libby. God sent you in my life as a blessing. Since the day our hearts met, my life has become truly amazing. I can't thank God enough for you. I look forward to growing old with you while watching our sons achieve great things, and then finally meeting God in His kingdom and spending our eternal lives together.

To my extremely talented and handsome sons, Ethan and Ivan, you two have filled my life with the utmost joy. I am so proud of, and will always love you both. I thank God every day for granting me the blessing of being your father. You have taught me so much, my sons. Please remember what your mother and I have taught you, and always respect everyone, even when you disagree with them, and God will always bless you.

To my mother, the most brilliant woman I know. Thank you for teaching me true patience, respect, and the importance of hard work. Thank you for making me a believer of God's miracles and showing me the importance of family. Who I am today, is because of you.

To my Grandpa, and my uncle Kabuchu, thank you for being the father figures in my life. Your constant support and encouragement has helped me achieve all that I have today.

To my family, you all are and have been my inspiration

throughout my life. I am thankful and humbled by your strong belief in me.

To my friends, you all are another true blessing in my life. I am thankful that you allowed me to share your lives, and the wisdom that flows through you is very important to me. You all truly are God sent. I am thankful for your continuous love, support, and friendship.

From birth I have relied on you; you brought me forth from my mother's womb. I will ever praise you...

—Psalm 71:6

INTRODUCTION

You have a roughly 1 in 150 million chance of being granted a visa to settle permanently in the United States. And, that's assuming you come from one of the "eligible" countries whose quota for available visas has not been met. With odds like that, those of you who have been approved a visa should consider yourselves some of the fortunate few.

My journey begins in 1993 in Kampala, the capital city of the small East African country of Uganda. A burly immigration official and I sat facing each other like adversaries in a chess match where only I could lose. Around us in the small office, stacks of folders lay on top of cracked wooden tables and rusty metal cabinets. Outside, uniformed guards with assault rifles and German Shepherd dogs paced around the perimeter. A faint odor of burning garbage drifted through the open windows. I was at the American consulate in a desperate bid to escape a life of extreme poverty in a tiny village in Western Uganda called Kyobugombe. Between me and freedom sat another human being with the authority to determine my fate.

A rattling fan on its full setting struggled in vain to grant solace from the heat. Sweat dribbled down my back as I leaned forward to pull my shirt away from sticking to my skin. The officer wiped his brow and thumbed through my application, scrawling notes along the margins. At that moment, I turned and squinted out of the window to avoid looking in his direction. I had to keep him from noticing my nervous blinking. Without glancing up, he reached across the desk and grabbed a rubber stamp. He flipped to the last page of my application and pressed the stamp across the signature line. As his hand pulled away from the surface, I shifted my gaze downward to see what impression the stamp had made. One word, bold and in bright red, sprang from the page.

DENIED!

I felt sick and light-headed. In that instant my hope of achieving a better life for me and my family in America vanished. I fought back the tears, and with hastened breathing fumbled at the application waved in my direction and shuffled out of the office. My family members were standing by in the dim hallway. The expression on my face betrayed my emotions. I heard a shallow gasp from someone in the group.

"What happened?" my uncle inquired, making an effort not to appear worried.

"He denied my application" I replied under my breath.

"Did he give you a reason why?"

"Not clearly. He asked me questions about travel arrangements, income, education, family members and such."

My uncle questioned me for several more minutes as we huddled in the shadows before we proceeded back out to the parking lot. We packed ourselves into a waiting rust bucket of a taxi and rolled out past the guard post onto the congested streets. After a short ride through the city we arrived at the busy bus terminal and within ten minutes hopped onto a departing bus.

The sun was setting as we began the six-hour drive back to the village. We rattled along dodging potholes and veering around matatus (taxi vans) stopped to pick up passengers. My uncle probed further about what took place. One statement I uttered captured his attention.

"The officer said what?" he queried, twisting in my direction with an earnest expression on his face.

"He said he doubted I would return to Uganda at the end of the visit," I stammered.

"Visit?" the tone of his voice pitched up. "We applied for you to migrate to America to settle with family members there, not to visit."

And there it was! At once we realized where the error lay. The officer had focused on whether or not I would be returning to Uganda, instead of viewing the paperwork as an application to emigrate to America. With that realization, the mood in the car shifted from somber to optimistic. We realized there was now a chance to reverse the outcome. We would appeal his decision. My goal of achieving the American dream was alive, but the road ahead would likely be bumpy and full of challenges.

My visa was eventually approved 1 year later, and after 2 decades of living in America I can finally say that I've achieved what many would consider "The American Dream". I learned a lot of lessons along the way and overcame numerous challenges. It occurred to me several years ago, however, that my path would have been a lot easier had there been some kind of manual available for how to go about this journey. While I appreciate everything I've gone through and really wouldn't change anything that happened in my life, I know it will be helpful to offer some actionable advice to others on this journey in the form of a Self Help book on how to Live the Dream.

For disclosure, this book is not about HOW to get to America, but about how to achieve the American Dream once you have arrived in America. I've been asked over the years by dozens of people interested in emigrating to America how exactly to go about this. For those of you who might have purchased this book hoping for a primer on how to get to America, I will devote a few paragraphs in this chapter to help with that. Keep in mind, however, that the rest of the book will not be oriented towards this topic.

There are some facts that aspiring immigrants should bear in mind. The September 11, 2001 terrorist attacks and the 2008 financial crisis were events that changed the landscape of immigration in the United States. The physical safety and financial security of Americans came under threat, and citizens demanded greater scrutiny of foreigners and a reduction in amounts and types of immigrants into the country. The result is a much more stringent application process and less wriggle room in the decision-making processes.

As far as the process is concerned, there are no shortcuts to coming to America. There are no bribes you can pay, people you can intimidate, processes you can skip, or connections you can take advantage of in order to get here. Attorneys can help you with filing your application, but they can't get it approved. Fraudsters can con you into paying a fee for entry, but they can't get you in. The only thing you can do is apply for a visa at a US embassy or consulate (https://www.usembassy.gov/) and it will be either approved or denied based solely on the merits of your particular case.

It helps to know what the various visa categories are before embarking on gathering the documents for your application and submitting. There are several non-immigrant and immigrant visa categories available that you may qualify for, as we shall display below.

Non-immigrant Visa Categories:

Athlete, amateur or professional.

Au pair (exchange visitor).

Australian professional specialty.

Border Crossing Card: Mexico.

Business visitor.

CNMI-only transitional worker.

Crew member.

Diplomat or foreign government official.

Domestic employee or nanny - must be accompanying a foreign national employer.

Employee of a designated international organization or NATO.

Exchange visitor.

Foreign military personnel stationed in the United States.

Foreign national with extraordinary ability in Sciences, Arts, Education, Business or Athletics.

Free Trade Agreement (FTA) Professional:

International cultural exchange visitor.

Intra-company transferee.

Medical treatment, visitor for.

Media, journalist.

NAFTA professional worker: Mexico, Canada.

Performing athlete, artist, entertainer.

Physician.
Professor, scholar, teacher (exchange visitor).
Religious worker.
Specialty occupations in fields requiring highly specialized knowledge.
Student: academic, vocational.
Temporary agricultural worker.
Temporary worker performing other services or labor of a temporary or seasonal nature.
Tourism, vacation, pleasure visitor.
Training in a program not primarily for employment.
Treaty trader/treaty investor.
Transiting the United States.
Victim of Criminal Activity.
Victim of Human Trafficking.
Non-immigrant (V) Visa for Spouse and Children of a Lawful Permanent Resident (LPR).
Immigrant Visa Categories:
Immediate Relative & Family Sponsored.
Spouse of a U.S. Citizen .
Spouse of a U.S. Citizen awaiting approval of an I-130 immigrant petition.
Fiancé(e) to marry U.S. Citizen & live in U.S.
Inter-country Adoption of Orphan Children by U.S. Citizens.
Certain Family Members of U.S. Citizens.
Certain Family Members of Lawful Permanent Residents.
Employer Sponsored – Employment
Employment-Based Immigrants, including (preference group):
Priority workers [First].

Professionals Holding Advanced Degrees and Persons of Exceptional Ability [Second].
Professionals and Other Workers [Third].
Employment Creation/Investors [Fifth].
Certain Special Immigrants: [Fourth].
Religious Workers.
Iraqi and Afghan Translators/Interpreters.
Iraqis Who Worked for/on Behalf of the U.S. Government.
Afghans Who Worked for/on Behalf of the U.S. Government.
Other Immigrants:
Diversity Immigrant Visa.
Returning Resident.

The process would begin with you ascertaining which of the above categories you best fit in, then going to the U.S. consulate in your country to collect the necessary application form(s). My particular visa fit under one of the immigrant visa categories. According to your category, you would gather all the documentation needed to satisfy the requirements and then submit your application for review. Keep in mind that there are direct and indirect costs involved with each submission (e.g., medical, fingerprinting, document handling, transportation, mailing, etc), and the review process itself could take months or even years with no guarantee of approval. In addition, errors in your submission could result in you needing to re-submit all your paperwork and start from the beginning.

Before you apply however, there are certain things you should know that are taken into account in the screening process. Knowing what those things are can help you prepare for your application before you submit it and increase your chances of being approved. Knowing these things can also help you determine the likelihood of success, and thereby save you from submitting an application that is most likely going to be denied, wasting your valuable money and resources.

The factors that are analyzed for each application include the following:

Anchors. Depending on your application type (whether you are applying to move to the US, attend school, just visit, etc), you must have strong physical, emotional, and financial ties either in America or back in your country of origin that will anchor you. These include a place of abode, a job or business, a source of income, family members, school, ties to or standing in the community, real estate property, investments, savings, etc. Obviously, some visa applications will not have all these requirements. For most of them, without strong anchors, your chances of approval are low. Lack of anchors is one of the most common reasons why people are denied entry into the United States.

Marital status. Are you single, married, common law? Being married to an American citizen is one of the most surefire ways of being approved to migrate to America. The marriage, however, must be genuine. This is an area that is heavily scrutinized due to the high levels of fraud involved. Taken into consideration are the circumstances of how and where you met, how long you were together before getting married, whether or not you had a wedding, how many family members from each side know each other, where and how you live, joint bank accounts, photo or video evidence of the two of you together, correspondence between each other, and much more.

Family ties. As with marital status, having a spouse, parent, or sibling who is a US citizen goes a long way towards increasing the chances of application approval. This is because there is a strong desire to keep or bring families together. In these cases, the petitioner should be the US citizen.

Criminal record. It goes without saying that if you have any kind of criminal record (checked through Interpol) your chances of approval drop to near zero. Unless you're squeaky clean in this area, don't bother applying.

Health status. As with having a criminal record, if at the time of your application a health screening reveals an illness or disease (particularly one that is communicable) your chances of approval will be diminished. Healthy individuals will not be a burden or threat to society, and will therefore receive some points in the 'approve' column in their favor.

Financial status/income/support. Whether you are intending to move to the US, attend school, or just visit, you must prove you can afford the cost of your visit, the cost of living here, or the costs of returning to your country of origin at the end of your schooling or visit. Funds in your or your sponsor's bank account will be checked. If you're moving here for a job, your offered salary will be taken into account in the application process. Some visa categories will not have a financial requirement.

Education level. For some categories, your education level will be taken into account in the application process. Up to a certain level and depending on the type of application, the more educated you are, the better your chances of approval (all other things considered).

Identification. The legitimate identity of the applicant is extremely important. The applicant's identity (yours and the petitioner's if it's not yourself) must be verified in the form of a driver's license, passport, birth certificate, national ID, etc. The more difficult it is to prove your identity, the lower the likelihood of approval.

References. Your application approval can be enhanced by references from people who know you and can vouch for your identity or reputation. These include family members, employers, schools, high ranking officials, prominent members of society, etc.

Age. There is a sweet spot for approval when it comes to age. Below and above a certain age, your chances of approval drop. Although not officially stated anywhere, you are generally considered a financial burden to your family and society when you are too young or too old to support yourself. People who can be productive citizens immediately and provide for themselves, their families, and their communities have a greater chance of being approved.

Fluency in English. How well you read, write, and comprehend the English language will be taken into account when you apply to migrate to America. Do as much as you can in this area before you submit your application. If an interview becomes necessary, the conversation that ensues will be for the purpose of establishing your fluency in the English language.

Profession. Although not a huge factor, your profession is also taken into account in the application process. In terms of being a productive citizen and contributing to society, your profession may win you some points if your area of specialization is one that the United States deems valuable.

Although not exhaustive, these are some of the factors that will be taken into account when you submit your application. Most applications will be denied on the basis of one or more of the above factors. If you're lucky enough to be approved, your journey to succeed in America will just be beginning.

The title of this book is "You Too Can Live The Dream: 10 Steps to Achieving The American Dream". The 10 steps have been broken up into, and are presented in, 10 individual chapters. For those of you living in the US, use the information laid out in each chapter to plot your journey, and my sincere hope is that you will find inside these pages a template for how you too can succeed in your quest to Live The American Dream.

CHAPTER 1

Integrating into a New Culture While Maintaining Your Roots

I leaped out of bed, startled by a rapid sequence of shrill beeps emanating from the shadows in the corner of the room. Scanning intently, I sighted a small clock radio on a bedside table with the time flashing in sync with the noise. Pulling the unit closer I observed a tiny knob along the top of the unit and snapped it to the off position to silence the cacophony. Disoriented from abruptly awakening out of a deep sleep, it took me several seconds to comprehend where I was. Last night I had completed a two-day trip from a small village in Western Uganda into the United States. I had spent the night at my uncle's place in a Maryland suburb just outside Washington D.C. It was 5:30 am. and I had just been rattled awake by an alarm clock. Amused and relieved, I doubled over in the center of the room and slapped my knee as the reality of the situation sank in. This sound was not the morning rooster call to which I was accustomed. A grin formed on my face, followed instantly by a burst of laughter.

Slices of sunlight streamed in through gaps in the shutters as I cracked open the door to see who else was awake. Listening intently, I could make out muffled voices filtering up from downstairs. I tiptoed forward toward the top of the stairs to hear if any of the voices were familiar. My uncle was speaking to somebody on the phone with the television set on in the background. Descending to the first level, I wandered into the empty kitchen and scanned the area to marvel at all the modern appliances.

It was impressive how all the items were placed safely and tidily off the floor in cabinets, on racks, and inside drawers. Seeing all the available silverware, I could not comprehend why there was a need for more than a few wooden spoons and a pair of saucepans to prepare all the food you needed. Shiny gadgets of all sorts lay along the counter. More electrical outlets were positioned along just the kitchen walls than I had seen in an entire dwelling in my village. The electric bill must be colossal, I thought.

Continuing to scan around the room, my eyes fixed upon the fridge in the corner. Having had an extended slumber, I was feeling famished. Opening the fridge door, I stared in wonder at the assortment of food, drinks, and condiments that filled the interior. Plastic containers stuffed with extras from yesterday's dinner sat on the shelves. I worked one loose from the stack, setting it on the counter. Upon hearing the fridge door opening and shutting my uncle came into the kitchen to announce good morning and show me how to use the microwave. I informed him I was used to eating cold leftovers in the morning. He prodded me to try warming up the food to determine if I preferred it that way.

Mid way through our conversation, my sister came bounding down the stairs, a bouncing ball of energy considering it was only a day after our exhausting flight. Hopping from foot to foot, she announced with much fanfare the trip to the flea market she would be taking with my uncle, and asked if I wanted to go along.

I pondered the offer for a few moments. Scenes of a village market played like a movie in my head.

"No thanks, you go ahead. I think I'll stick around here to rest up and get myself oriented."

"Okay, suit yourself. Don't be jealous when you see all the marvelous things I pick up for cheap though," she boasted.

I shrugged and dug another mouthful of food out of the container. Today was my first day in America and I was eager to look around the house and possibly walk around the neighborhood. My uncle, a reserved and mannerly gentleman, gave me an overview of things around the house so I could take advantage of my time alone without damaging items or injuring myself. He notified me that everyone had left early for work, school, or errands and I would be by myself until later that afternoon. I assured him I would be fine then escorted them out the door as they started out to do their shopping.

Outside was frigid, so I darted back into the warm house and began assessing my situation. For such a long time I had dreamed of living in America, and now that I was here I had no inkling what to do first or how to establish my next step. I sat down on the couch to put together a plan of action. To start with, I was weary of being startled each time I encountered something new. I was going to have to expect things to be unfamiliar, and would have to use each opportunity to learn about myself as well as the new environment. Next, I would need to figure out how to earn an income so as not to depend on family members for any longer than necessary.

With a rough plan somewhat formed in my head, I made my way around the house peering into each room that was unlocked. The place was spacious, with enough rooms to accommodate seven to eight people. For the first time in my life, I had my own bedroom, and inside it a proper bed in which to sleep. Washing up would no longer be done outdoors using a basin. There would be no need to chop firewood or fetch water from a nearby river. Needing to use the toilet would not require a walk to the outhouse. And where did people keep their mosquito nets?

This pattern kept up for several months. Each day and week I discovered and marveled at something new. Sidewalks. Cable television. Air conditioning. Manicured lawns. Skyscrapers. Escalators. Car washes. Jean shorts. Two lane highways. 24-hour stores. Hot water in the taps. Valentine's Day. Commuter trains. Overpasses. Garbage trucks. Electric razors.

Then, one day, it happened. I was getting ready to go to work, and in the silence of the empty house I felt alone. Nobody was around, not even the neighbors out in their front yards. Even when they were there, I didn't care about them, and I felt they didn't care about me. Compared to the spirit of community found in the villages, this pull-yourself-up-by-the-bootstraps individualism in America suddenly felt cold and selfish. Looking around, unused appliances scattered throughout the house appeared wasteful and unnecessary. Ways of doing things seemed odd, and I was feeling more and more out of place in more and more situations. One thing after another appeared not to make sense, and I was starting to miss "home".

The main problem I was having was attempting to reconcile everything I had seen in movies and television shows about "the West" with what was actually transpiring around me. In the movies, everybody was successful as long as they worked hard and maintained high ethical standards. Only the lazy and criminal-minded among the population ended up unaccomplished and discontented. Yet here I was, feeling empty and frustrated at the meager prospects that lay before me. I kept thinking that somehow I was to blame for my inability to instantly succeed in a land where simply showing up landed you at the finish line. I also felt I was letting down all those people in the village who had bid me well wishes and God's speed in the face of all the hardship they were being left to endure.

Furthermore, I was finding many interactions between myself and non-immigrants to be fake and superficial. Some people I interacted with reacted to me with fear, disgust, and suspicion, even accusing me of coming to America to bring disease, steal their jobs, and change the American culture to a different one they would no longer recognize or want to be part of. Some muttered under their breath but within hearing distance that they were becoming the minority in their own country. Encounters with others would be brief, with nothing more than a quick "hello, how was your day?" and as little communication as necessary before moving on. Me being a quiet and shy individual didn't help matters much, and I often failed to understand some of the phrases that were being uttered to me anyway. All in all, I was beginning to wonder if coming to America had been the wisest decision I could have made considering all the costs associated with the petition and move.

Eventually, I recovered from this phase and settled smoothly into day-to-day life. In the many years since that tough period, I have come to realize that there were several phases I went through while trying to integrate into American society. The stages I went through closely resemble those described by Gregory Trivonovitch, a researcher and Associate Director of the Culture Learning Institute at the East-West Center in Hawaii. I managed to go through all these stages and make a good life for myself and my family, while some immigrant friends of mine failed to integrate and ended up returning to their countries of origin. While going through the process, I also found it important to maintain some of my roots and add some of that flavor into my everyday life as a way of making a contribution. Following are some suggestions to help you make it smoothly through the necessary transition.

This Chapter's Takeaways

There are 4 phases you will likely go through, and need to go through, in order to transition successfully as an immigrant in the United States:

The Honeymoon Phase

The Crash Phase

The Recovery Phase

The Integration Phase

The first phase you will likely go through when you first arrive in America is the Honeymoon phase. In this phase, everything you perceive and experience will feel wonderful. You will be so happy to finally be in America, the land of milk and honey, where anything is possible and the streets are paved with gold. Some things may appear strange, but nonetheless exciting. Making snowmen in December will be a thrill. The hustle and bustle of the big city will feel electric. Everything will be an adventure, with something new to discover around every corner. All things bad in your country of origin will be good here. You will be happy to encounter unfamiliar situations and be willing to learn things from the culture that are contemporary and forward-thinking. This phase can last anywhere from a few weeks to several months. Depending on the particular circumstances of your case, some of you may remain in this phase permanently.

The next phase is the Crash phase. In this phase, suddenly things you may have ignored or failed to perceive in the Honeymoon phase will begin to come into focus. You may start to miss your family members, colleagues, schoolmates, or friends left behind in your country of origin. Certain customs or ways of life may start to appear strange and unwanted, depending on your cultural background. You may miss certain elements of your previous lifestyle and culture. Some of you may experience racism, prejudice, or sexism you didn't expect to encounter. The wonderful life you thought you would be living in America may suddenly appear out of reach, or simply to be a mirage. Opportunities you thought would be readily available to you may now seem illusive. Disappointment, depression, hopelessness, frustration, or anger may set in. Depending on the particular circumstances of your arrival, a number of you may skip this Crash phase altogether. For an unfortunate few, finding a way out of the Crash phase may prove to be elusive, resulting in a return to your country of origin. For the rest, this phase can last from a few weeks to several months.

The next phase is the Recovery phase. This is where you strive to recover from the crash you've been experiencing. Strategies include making frequent phone or Skype/WhatsApp calls to family members and friends "back home", or corresponding by mail. You may need to find locations where people with similar backgrounds frequent. Conversely, there may be places where or people whom you seek to avoid. Ask your American friends and colleagues questions about the things that you find confusing or don't understand. Talk to other immigrants who have succeeded in settling comfortably into society about your feelings. Set goals and a course which helps you find a purpose. Do things that build your self-esteem and self-worth. Develop hobbies and find activities you enjoy doing. Research school or career options. Attend church or see a counselor. Create and follow diligently an exercise routine, and pay close attention to your nutrition. Yoga or meditation might help some, while vitamin supplements or medication might help others. Depending on the type of visa you hold, a trip back to your country of origin for a quick visit might help.

Whatever you do, though, resist developing a bunker mentality where you only interact with people from your country of origin. It's not unusual to find in many major cities Hispanic, Chinese, European, African, or Caribbean immigrants clustered in their segregated ethnic communities for comfort and stability. These communities often have names like "Chinatown", "Little Italy", "Little Haiti", etc. In some cases, many of those immigrants feel they've simply been driven into those neighborhoods by hostility from the native population. Residential segregation hinders integration, so do not retreat into such isolation.

Worse yet, avoid retreating into dark corners and interacting with radical individuals who can fill your head with negative thoughts. This will not aid in your recovery and integration process, and will instead leave you much less a part of the American culture you're trying to integrate into.

The length of the recovery phase will depend on your particular resources and willingness to overcome and succeed. A few of you will never enter the Crash phase and therefore will have no need for a recovery phase. Some of you may enter and unfortunately never recover from the crash. Others of you may recover for some period of time (months or even years) only to crash again. Some of you may cycle through these phases several times throughout your life in America. For most, however, you will spend your time in the recovery phase utilizing strategies like those above that will help you to stabilize.

The final phase is the Integration phase. Once you enter this phase, it will mean you have gone through the growing pains of the crash and can begin the journey to achieve living the American dream. In this phase, you will have stabilized and figured out the things you need to do in order to integrate into society. You will have figured out the meaning of phrases you didn't understand, made sense of the way people behaved and interacted, and deciphered the cultural norms and ways of going about doing things.

One of the surest ways to integrate smoothly into the culture is to invest heavily in learning to read, write, speak, and comprehend English. You can do this by signing up for language classes and speaking English as often and in as many situations as possible. Any time you hear a word you don't understand, stop and ask what it means. Your socioeconomic status will greatly be shaped by your English language acquisition. This will be your key to unlocking the full potential of the American Dream and breaking down some of the barriers that might stand in your way. Your progress will be extremely limited if you can't communicate effectively with people. Many things are lost in translation, and the likelihood of being defrauded by hucksters is high if you don't understand what is being said. You need to be able to understand road signs, negotiate contracts, investigate career options, read menus, attend schools, conduct job interviews, interact with customers and colleagues, follow directions, decipher instructions, serve on a jury, make sense in an argument, and so much more. The more you can master the English language, the better you can integrate and the more benefits you can avail yourself of.

Another important element that will help you in the integration process is to learn what the American cultural norms and values are. Learning can sometimes be a tricky thing because America is essentially a country of immigrants, with most Americans tracing their ancestry to immigrants. Therefore, the cultural norms and values have developed over time and mean something slightly different now than they did one hundred years ago. However, some things you might pick up about American culture include, for example, a frank and direct way of speaking, a rugged individualism, an expectation to pull yourself up from your station, a respect for the rule of law, a sense of optimism, a "can-do" spirit, a striving for excellence, an orientation towards the future, an appetite for self-improvement, and more. Find ways to weave some of these cultural values into your daily life.

Another way to integrate into the American culture is to participate in the political system by, among other things, voting. Being part of the process of electing local, state, and national officials makes you feel like you are integrated into the society in which you live. Holding representatives accountable for their actions gives you a sense of power that overrides any feelings of hopelessness or worthlessness you may have. This in turn energizes you and provides you with a feeling that you are somebody that matters in the big picture. Preparing to vote also opens up avenues of conversation between yourself and citizens around you, aiding in practicing your social skills and transitioning into the new culture.

Keep in mind that integration can be aided or hampered to a large extent by the majority non-immigrant "host" community into which you may be immersed. This means that, despite what was mentioned earlier, it can sometimes be easier to start the integration process living in regions with a high concentration of immigrants from a similar background as you than it is in a community of non-immigrants. When for example you go to the bank, take a trip to your local grocery store, visit the neighborhood cafe, attend church, or drop your kids off at school, members of the community will feel less threatened if they've interacted with other people who look or act like you. Being the different one makes you stand out, and most people are uncomfortable around others who are much unlike themselves. The point of integration, however, is to not stay in these pockets forever. Take the time to integrate, and once you've learned the cultural norms and values and can blend into society like a member of the majority group (mainly by speaking English fluently, acting "proud to be American", respecting the rule of law, and maintaining legal status, for example), then it makes it easier to navigate your way out into different communities.

While integrating, it is important to maintain some of your roots and find ways to incorporate things from your culture into your new environment. This balance can help you settle comfortably into a way of life that is sustainable and productive. This can also help to reduce some of the hostility you may encounter with native members of the population. America is, after all, a melting pot where people from all over the world migrate to; so you should make efforts to contribute something new to the culture that complements but does not disrespect all that is unique about the great American experiment.

Things that you can maintain from your culture and contribute to American society include music, art, clothing/fashion, poetry, paintings, crafts, cuisine, innovation, etc. You can introduce some of these to your friends and colleagues at parties or events where you have a chance to tell them a little bit about the history and culture of the items. If you are well motivated and financed you can even open up a restaurant, retail shop or gallery that offers these cultural contributions to the general public. Another thing you can introduce to the culture is your unique perspective on issues and challenges. Historically, challenging problems have been solved, and important discoveries made, by looking in from a different perspective. Learning that your culture can add value to the inventory of ideas or foster innovation can help dissolve the myth that immigrants are only here to take, and have nothing to offer or put on the table. This helps in the two way street aspect of the integration process.

Your journey to achieve the Dream may be long, but it will be fruitful if you utilize the strategies in this chapter and the rest of the book to make it successfully through the different phases. Hopefully, this chapter has given you good insight into the process of integrating into the new culture while maintaining your roots.

CHAPTER 2

Avoiding Pitfalls and Overcoming Challenges

I was part of a two-man crew working as a house cleaner for a large American cleaning company. For the ninth day in a row, I was making my way through the Maryland suburbs on the way to a customer's house, feeling slightly embarrassed at the large decal on the car door announcing our profession. My co-worker and I were engaging in the usual banter about all the things we wished we were doing rather than cleaning. Out of nowhere, he snapped his head in my direction and asked me to open the glove compartment and pull out a small bag stashed within. I complied and handed it over to him.

"You wanna try some of this?" he asked, shaking the bag in my face.

"Some of what?" I replied naively.

"Let's just say it's an illicit drug, one I think you would like if you tried. You need to loosen up and have some fun"

I was instantly both horrified and terrified. What if we got pulled over by the cops right now? I would definitely go to jail just for being in the same vehicle as him whether or not the drugs were mine. Furthermore, this was my reckless co-worker and I had no idea how much trouble he would get me into if I continued to hang around with him. I shook my head while trying not to look in his direction and muttered something incomprehensible about not wanting to get caught. We made it the rest of the way to the client's home without incident. The following day I asked my supervisor to pair me with another partner operating in a different part of the state. He asked the reason why and I simply stated we didn't get along very well and my performance was being affected.

In a few months I grew tired of getting rides from my co-worker or taking the bus to and from work, so after some driving lessons with my uncle I decided to buy my own car. I had saved $4,500 from my second cleaning job and decided I would use this to buy a used vehicle. On my way to work on several occasions the previous week I had seen a car parked at the side of the road with a 'For Sale' sign placed in the windshield. Today was my day off so I took the bus a few blocks from home to the spot and hopped off to take down the phone number. I dialed the digits and a gentleman answered, agreeing to come over immediately to see about negotiating a price for the car. After 30 minutes or so, he arrived and we agreed on a price of $4,500 cash. I was elated to own my first vehicle, a golden Chevy Spectrum.

A few days later, I was driving to the mall to run some errands when the car suddenly stalled. A strong stench of fuel filled the air, and when I got out to open the hood I noticed a trail of liquid on the road behind me. It appeared fuel had been leaking from the car since I had left the house. A helpful employee at a nearby pizzeria offered to call a tow truck, and one arrived within an hour to tow the car to a garage. Upon arrival and inspection it was revealed that besides leaking fuel, there was a problem with the vehicles' carburetor. I received a quote for the fix and then took a bus home.

The next day I had scraped together barely enough for the repairs so I was forced to walk over an hour to the garage to pick up the car. It was a scorching hot day, and along the way I flagged down a passing pickup truck and asked for a ride. The driver kindly agreed and I hopped into the back along with my sister. We arrived at the garage 20 minutes later. Upon walking up to the counter, I reached into my pocket to remove my wallet and to my dismay found it missing. I rushed outside but by then the pickup truck had driven away and I didn't have the driver's phone number to call him. My car had been repaired and was available to be picked up, but I couldn't drive it off the lot without paying. An impassioned plea to the busy garage owner fell on sympathetic but deaf ears. An employee just completing his shift felt sorry and offered us a ride home, but on the way out I was informed there would be a storage fee levied for each day the vehicle remained on the lot.

Upon my return, one week's worth of storage fees had been added to the cost of the repairs, since that's how long it had taken for me to get my next paycheck and borrow from family members. Two days after picking up the car from the lot, my wallet appeared in the mail with everything inside except the cash. Six months later the car broke down for the final time, and I was back on the bus or getting rides from friends, family members, and co-workers to get to and from work. The pitfalls and challenges continued to present themselves, and for each one I overcame, I became a stronger and wiser person.

Many years and challenges later, I made the bold decision to join the US military as a way to give back for all that I had attained. After much research and preparation, the day arrived for me to leave for training. Even though I was ready, it felt very difficult to leave my pregnant wife alone with a 2-year old active son. We prayed and hugged for a long time. I finally got into my recruiter's uniform with the Army Strong Logo on it, and headed for the BWI airport to Missouri. There, our handlers were waiting for the fresh new recruits. We boarded the bus that took us to the processing unit where all new comers are processed into the system.

The first day was great... nice and easy, as were the following couple of days. A few days later, however, we were introduced to our drill sergeants, a group of patriotic yet stern individuals who assured us with a single glance that they meant business. As the processing began, we were told to take our clothes off and put them in bags that would be sent home to our families. We were then instructed to walk from station to station wearing nothing but our newly issued army brown underwear.

After 5 days of this we were ready for the official boot camp. Early in the morning, we were lined up and briefed on the journey to our final training company... 495 Delta. Each of us had two fully packed duffle bags - one worn in the front and the other in the back - and one backpack in our right hands. Our transportation was a cattle truck with no seats and a few poles to grab on when needed. We boarded and crammed ourselves in the available space. As soon as the truck began to move, the drill sergeants pounced aboard and began walking on our shoulders. According to them we had left no space for them to walk in the cattle truck. One of them stomped on my shoulder. I felt myself about to buckle under the weight, but was grateful that he stayed there for just about a second as they were moving up and down in the truck yelling obscenities I had never heard used in the English language before.

I could not wait to get out of that truck and get some fresh air, and to get away from all the yelling. But, I was kidding myself. Things had not even started yet. After about 40 minutes in the cattle truck, we arrived at our destination. These buildings would be our official residences for the next 6-7 months. We would be given exactly 3 minutes to do most everything. For each thing we failed to do in the allotted time we were punished with corrective training. This would involve doing push-ups, sit-ups, low crawls, high crawls until many of us in the group of about 140 male and female candidates all together started to have muscle failure. On one occasion I fell on my face in fatigue attempting a set of push-ups. One of the drill sergeants yelled in my face that she had never seen a weaker guy than me in her entire career.

A few mornings later I was standing by my bunk bed with my hand on my hip.

"You think you're in charge?" bellowed a drill sergeant, sprinting to get to within an inch of my face.

"No, drill sergeant" I stammered.

"Well, you're standing there like you think you're in charge. If that's the case, here is something you will be in charge of" he announced, spinning around and grabbing a fire extinguisher from the wall.

And with that, I was to be in charge of carrying this around with me everywhere I went for several days. The instructions were very clear; both of my hands had to stay on the fire extinguisher, day and night. My battle buddy, an individual each soldier is paired with for the duration of training, hated me for it. This was because if, for example, I had to ease myself, my battle buddy would have to hold the fire extinguisher for me. Any activity that required me to use my two hands, my battle buddy had to take over the fire extinguisher. We made it through the time sore and bruised.

One day, one of the fellow recruits left his shoe shining kit visible under his bunk bed. We came back from a long training session to find the entire platoon barracks painted in black shoe shine. All the wall lockers were pushed down on the floor and some thrown out of the window. As usual, we were given 3 minutes to clean the barracks and have everything inspection ready for the first Sergeant. Inspection ready meant bunk beds lined up, uniforms neatly placed in wall lockers or wardrobes with an inch in between each hanger, socks folded and lined up in a specific way, underwear folded in a certain manner and stacked up uniformly on shelves in the wall locker, barracks swept and buffed, and no markings on the walls like shoe polish. We barely got a fraction of all of these things done before the Sergeant came for inspection. The punishment for failure was to go and exercise in the swamp with our full combat gear on, which consisted of rucksacks containing 45 pounds of gear and our training weapons. Many of us ended up going to sick call after it was all said and done.

Finally, those of us who survived ended up graduating from Advanced Individual Training, also referred to as AIT. The evaluation I received from my senior drill sergeant was one of the best I've received in my entire life. This came to me as a surprise because there had been no hint of such an outcome during training. What impressed me further is that all the challenges I overcame ultimately made me a stronger and better person.

In undertaking the journey to achieve the American Dream you will likely encounter tough situations. These will indeed help to shape and mold the person you end up becoming, so you must find a way to embrace these challenges and grow from them.

This Chapter's Takeaways

Following is some advice I would like to give about avoiding pitfalls while overcoming challenges:

Recognize that something in front of you is a challenge, and that overcoming it involves strategies or information gathering that will make you a better version of yourself. Attempting to avoid obstacles or challenges will likely leave you a lesser version of yourself since you won't grow by applying strategic critical thinking. Take on challenges, and the things you learn from the process will benefit you in the long run.

Use history to your advantage. If you've tackled something similar before, apply some of the lessons learned from the past to your current situation. When I purchased my first vehicle for example, it annoyed me later how I didn't negotiate the price and ended up paying the gentleman all the money I had, even though I came from a country where everything was negotiated. I didn't use history to my advantage and ended up (over)paying the price.

Believe that you can achieve your goal of overcoming the challenge. This belief will increase your motivation to solve your problem. With strong belief, you can go ahead and invest the time, resources, and commitment necessary to overcome your challenge. Without belief, you will struggle to put forth the energy required and likely fall short of overcoming the particular challenge that lies in front of you. This in turn will destroy your self-esteem and make you less likely to make attempts to steer clear of pitfalls in the future. Keep in mind that you will need to set goals that you believe can be achieved in the first place.

Utilize what you have within your control, and let go of the rest. Things that are out of your control include politics, the weather, other people's attitudes, etc. For example, in the army it was painfully clear that my drill sergeants far outranked me and controlled everything while we were in training. I had to let go of what I couldn't control and stick to what was in my control, like my faith, emotions, stamina, concentration, attitude, and so on. It would have been infinitely frustrating to attempt to control anything beyond whatever was within my control. I was able to utilize what was within my control and get through the physical and mental challenges in front of me.

Pick your battles. Tackle a challenge or address an issue only if it is in the way of you achieving your ultimate goal. Otherwise, you will end up wasting resources and time dealing with something that could have just been avoided altogether. Some challenges I had to abandon simply because they were not worth the fight. One I remember painfully is when we moved into our third house pending the sale of our previous one. When we were unable to sell it, we rented it out. The renter ended up being a deadbeat, and for 2 years we paid the mortgage on 2 homes, stretching our finances very thin. While we could have fought the tenant and tried to sue them in court for rent arrears, we instead opted to sell the house for less than we owed the bank just to free ourselves from the ordeal.

Integrate flexibility into planning. It's great to plan for challenges and have strategies to avoid pitfalls, but maintaining flexibility will go a long way to you achieving success. The best laid plans have ways of unraveling, so being flexible with solutions will help you more frequently than being rigid.

Look for, and recognize solutions around you. Many times, when you find yourself confronting a challenge, the options available seem limited to what you have and know. Sometimes a solution is right in front of you or around you but you fail to see it and take advantage. Learn to recognize resources you can tap into to help solve your problems.

Seek advice and support from trustworthy people around you. An underutilized resource in times of challenge is your network of trustworthy friends and family members. Most likely, people around you have encountered some of the problems you might be facing, and getting insight from others can help you formulate a plan and get yourself out of a tough situation. Also, getting second opinions about strategies you might be considering employing can be useful.

Focus on the solution, not the blame. Often times when we arrive at a pitfall or encounter a challenge, the temptation is to look for who to blame for our predicament. Focusing on blame takes energy and resources away from finding a solution. It's always best to spend time developing a solution or fix to the problem, and once you've stabilized, only then debriefing to unpack what happened so you can avoid falling into the same hole. Being in the army taught me very clearly that in the heat of things, the solution is infinitely more important than the blame.

Don't let negative emotions take over the situation. Doing so can leave you paralyzed and unable to come up with solutions to the problems you're facing. If you drown in negative emotions you will feel like everything is hopeless and there is no point trying to overcome the challenges ahead. Also, your self-esteem will be crushed, which is something you need to have in full amounts to tackle what's in front of you. Keep these negative thoughts at bay and you will be able to move forward.

Accept any necessary change quickly. The longer you take to accept the fact that you might need to make a change in your course, the longer it will take to begin working on the right solution. You only have a limited amount of time and resources available, so burning through the few resources you have while heading in the wrong direction is wasteful. Realizing when a change of strategy was necessary, I've managed to accomplish many more things in my life than most of my friends and colleagues have managed in the same amount of time. I tend to move quickly, and if any change is necessary, I do so without too much hesitation.

Don't be afraid to make the wrong decision. Whenever we face a pitfall or challenge, we're often afraid to make a move that might end up being the wrong one. If you take that approach you won't make any decision at all and end up stuck in the same place. Even the smartest people in the world have made a wrong decision at some point in their career, yet that has not prevented them from becoming a success. Part of making a decision involves potentially making a mistake, so this is unavoidable. Put lots of thought and research into your decision, and once you feel comfortable enough with it, make your move.

Consider the worst-case scenario. When faced with a challenge or problem, we are often terrified and paralyzed by the worst-case scenario. If, for example, we don't like our job, we are terrified that we might not be able to find another suitable one if we quit. This makes us steer away from seeking a solution, and keeps us trapped where we don't want to be. Considering the worst-case scenario, and being okay with it, frees us to develop strategies that can mitigate any downsides associated with the necessary changes.

Steer clear of the naysayers. Avoid the people around you who do nothing but criticize any decision you make. These naysayers can also steer you in the wrong direction or tempt you with distractions that pull you away from your goal. I had naysayers from all the way back home who didn't believe I would amount to anything if I moved to the United States, or who thought leaving my high school before graduating was the wrong thing to do. Once I arrived, I faced more naysayers who tried to dissuade me from pursuing higher education. People like this can get in the way of you finding solutions to problems you're facing, so avoid them or move away from them in order to move forward.

Break the problem or challenge up into smaller, more manageable pieces. A problem can appear insurmountable if you look at it from the perspective of the whole piece. Split the problem up into pieces, then develop strategies to solve one piece at a time. Doing this will make solving the problem more manageable, and will provide you the confidence you need to tackle the challenge over time. Develop short-term, medium-term, and long-term goals that you can meet in order to solve your problem.

When facing a challenge that seems insurmountable or unbearable, always keep in mind that "this too shall pass". Doing so prevents you from being paralyzed by the burden of the problem and not making it seem like the challenge will overtake your life. Once you understand that the problem or challenge can be temporary, you free yourself up to develop winning strategies.

Put all the available options on the table and look for creative solutions. Most of us have a general worldview from which we analyze problems and look for answers. Sometimes the solution can only be seen from a different perspective, or even crystallize itself when looked at from another angle. Even if you end up with the solution you preferred, scratching off all the other available ones gives you confidence that you left no stone unturned while researching your option.

Seek out others who have overcome the challenge you're facing. Undoubtedly, you are not the first person on the planet to encounter the particular challenge you're facing. Surely, others have faced it too, and finding and talking to them can help you come up with strategies to overcome the problem or avoid the pitfall.

Articulate your challenge or problem clearly. People around you, especially loved ones and friends, may not understand the challenge you are facing if you are unable to explain it to them in a manner that makes sense. This can lead to friction, misunderstanding, or frustration from the very people that can offer you some assistance or allow you space to deal with the issue at hand. Expressing yourself clearly also helps you see the problem in its full light and enables you to begin strategizing a solution.

Visualize your solution. After you craft and execute a solution to a particular problem or challenge, visualize the solution any time you find yourself slipping backwards or getting discouraged. It's often difficult to know if your solution is working when the results aren't immediate, so sticking to the plan will require you to see what the end result is even before it happens. This will also help you stay motivated to continue putting in the hard work in times of difficulty.

These strategies, among others, will help you avoid pitfalls and overcome challenges as you go through your journey to live your dream.

CHAPTER 3

Obtaining a Solid Education and Acquiring Financial Literacy

One of the schools I attended in Uganda was Kigezi High School (KHS), the most prestigious in the Western region of the country. I had struggled at my former school of Rwesasi Primary School, where classes were taught in the Runyankole Rukiga dialect and English was not introduced to me until the fourth grade. On a second attempt, I produced a score just high enough to attend KHS. Keeping up was tough because students in this school were extremely studious and disciplined. Indeed, the school had produced many illustrious alumni as a result of this study ethic. Today I felt like sleeping in, but the punishment for being late was a flogging that would leave marks for days and make it painful to sit. Knowing what could be in store, I dashed outside to wash. Then I hopped into my only uniform and ran to school barefoot. Arriving with time to spare, I joined my classmates in sweeping the floor then sat at my desk to begin the school day.

In class I was shy and rarely spoke. Indeed, some classmates thought I was speech-impaired. Giving an incorrect answer to a question or making errors while reading were transgressions deserving of a spanking, so I took notes diligently and tried to avoid being called upon to make a presentation. After a couple of hours of instruction and study, we were let out of class for the morning recess. Most of the students used this time to dash home for lunch, but since there was seldom food at home I walked to a nearby river and passed the allotted time sitting at the edge. In desperate times when I could tolerate it, I would line up with other students for the provided lunch of posho (maize floor cooked in a solid form) and beans, which occasionally contained dead weevils in it. Later, I joined a few friends in my dormitory to break-dance to our favorite Zouk/Lingala music. Boys from our dormitory were known throughout the school for our dancing abilities, in addition to discipline, cleanliness, athleticism, and having the best kept flowers.

While dancing in the narrow hallways, a group of older boys began pestering me as they frequently did, trying to force me to sing songs with the most embarrassing lyrics imaginable. I usually delighted in singing, but not to these types of songs. Yet I acquiesced out of fear. These same boys were to patrol the dormitories in the dead of night, beating up the smallest among us and confiscating anything they wished during their rounds of terror. As one of the scrawniest in the class, I planned to escape the drama by spending the night at a relatives' home as I routinely did. A few classmates would join me in evading the wrath of the tormentors. Such was school life for me in Uganda.

Several years later, I was in the United States living with relatives in the state of Maryland. While working as a cleaner for minimum wage in two separate companies it occurred to me that I would be stuck in this type of dead-end job unless I furthered my education. I noticed that almost all the people in upper management positions at these companies had college degrees of some kind while those of us stuck hunched over on all fours cleaning all day had none. I needed to do something about this, but was facing plenty of discouragement from people around me about the prospect of going to college. Some said I wasn't smart enough or thought I was better than them, and others said I couldn't afford it, while others wished me to continue working and applying the income I was receiving towards paying bills.

Eventually, I could no longer stand all the negativity and decided to be bold and make an attempt to attend school despite the naysayers. One morning, after discovering information in the local yellow pages directory, I hopped on a bus to a nearby facility of Wheaton High School. Upon arriving and talking to a guidance counselor, I was informed that I was too old to attend. The counselor advised me to take the GED (General Equivalency Diploma) test instead, which would serve as a pathway to attending college. I signed up immediately and soon thereafter began taking evening classes to prepare for the test, which I eventually passed. With the GED in hand I was able to attend a number of institutions of higher learning and opportunity, including AccuTech Business Institute, Montgomery College, Potomac College, Hood College, Kaplan University, and the United States Army.

In the early stages of my college years a major cause of stress and anxiety for me was selecting a major. Although my initial interests were to go for either a pharmacy program or a veterinarian program, it was a struggle balancing my interests with my career aspirations. Just like many other students, I had no clear idea about my passion and whether what I wanted to do would make a good career choice. I went through a lot of stress deciding which program to select until I received some guidance from my teachers and some good friends of mine. Once I came to the understanding that picking a college major isn't necessarily a lifetime commitment, it became a lot easier for me to make a decision. I learned that I would always have an option of changing my major or switching my career. From the institutions I received a Medical Office Administration Certificate, a Bachelor of Science in Information Systems Management (BSM), a Military Police (31B) Certificate, a Master of Business Administration (MBA) Information Systems concentration, and a Master of Public Health (MPH).

I can personally tell you that education is the most important part in achieving stability in today's world, whether you live in a country with many opportunities or in one of the poorest countries on Earth. An education can be obtained formally from a learning institution, informally by "just doing it" or learning on the job, and by interning, apprenticing, or volunteering. The path you choose will depend on your particular passions or abilities as well as available financing opportunities. There are many good reasons for you to obtain a solid education and acquire financial literacy which I will now cover.

This Chapter's Takeaways

First, particularly in the United States, there is a direct correlation between education level and earning potential. More educated people generally earn higher incomes than their less educated counterparts. Being well qualified to do your job gives you a sense of satisfaction and builds your self-esteem in a way that helps you stay healthier and happier. Possessing high levels of competence puts you in a good position for a long career of salary raises and job promotions.

Second, attending school helps you develop additional skills such as self-discipline, time-keeping, social interaction, and communication. Social skills enable us to develop good relationships and build a solid support system. Communication skills help us to reason through challenging scenarios and avoid resorting to violence, for example. These skills can be put to use in all aspects of your life beyond the campus environment.

Third, attending school enables you to develop networks or connections that can assist you with job openings or other income-generating or career enhancing opportunities. Having a referral from somebody inside a company that attended school with you can be a huge leg up in your quest to get a job or promotion.

Fourth, in the event of a layoff, being educated allows you to utilize knowledge and skills to find ways to generate income or get employed that do not involve criminal activity. Staying out of the criminal justice system is one of the crucial elements that help you achieve the American Dream.

The important thing to keep in mind, however, is to be careful about going into massive debt in the form of student loans in order to obtain a degree with little earning potential. Carefully evaluate the prospects of earning a high enough income to pay back the loans from your career choice.

Along with a good education you also need to possess solid financial literacy. Financial literacy is knowing how to manage your personal financial life, including both day-to-day as well as long term planning. Areas of financial literacy include budgeting, saving, tax filing and planning, insurance, investing, tuition, debt management, social security and retirement planning, real estate, and more. Being financially literate helps you evaluate whether any purchase you intend to make is required, affordable, and an asset or a liability. Being knowledgeable also helps you avoid falling into situations that are against your best financial interest; like predatory lending, high interest rate loans, fraud, etc. You will also see it as a priority to maintain a good credit rating while avoiding bankruptcy or foreclosure.

Connecting Your Education to Your Career Choices

Based on my experience and understanding, here are a few additional tips for those of you looking to go to college that I personally used which can help you determine the right college major and the right career path for you:

Start Considering your Hobbies

The first thing you need to do is to consider your hobbies and write them all down. Think of the reasons you enjoy these activities. For instance, if you are into arts and craft, maybe it's because you like creating unique things. You can perhaps opt for a career in graphic designing.

Seek Help through Career Resource Center

There are career resource centers present in the majority of the colleges in America. These are perfect places to seek information and conduct research about any career imaginable. Once you find careers of interest you can determine what training or skills would be required.

Talk to a Career Counselor

Talking to a career counselor can help in clearing your mind and assisting you in finding the right career path. You may even learn about careers you never knew existed.

Career Tests

Your career counselor might suggest you to take certain tests to help guide you towards your areas of interest. There are plenty of career assessment tests available for you to take. However, if you are opting to take tests online then you must be cautious as many of them are unreliable. The best thing to do is to take these tests under the guidance of your career counselor.

Interview Professionals

Perhaps there are several careers that you find interesting. If so, you can choose the best one of them by interviewing professionals who are already in those fields. Conduct a quick informational interview either over the phone or in person. Ask relevant questions that will help you gain exposure to their field or work. There are many professionals out there who will be happy to help young individuals establish their career choices.

Start Shadowing Someone

After you have conducted those interviews, ask the professionals who you believe have the most intriguing careers if you can shadow them for a day or two. This will give you an even clearer idea about what a typical day in that career would be like. Doing so can enable you to learn about other jobs associated with that field that may interest you even more than your original choice.

Do an Internship

If you find the job interesting after shadowing someone for a day, then it is a good idea to attempt to get a summer job or an internship at the company. This will help you gain some work experience and may even open a door to a future job. If your degree qualifies you for a range of different positions, for instance a business degree, then internships will help you in narrowing down your choices and enable you to develop skills that will be useful.

Start Volunteering

If it's not possible for you to commit to an internship for several months then try volunteering. You will still learn plenty about the profession but will have the choice of leaving it early if you don't like it.

Don't Be Afraid

If you are interested in finding the best career path for you, it is imperative that you not be afraid. You must be confident enough to make some phone calls, ask questions, or shadow someone in order to learn more. Being afraid or anxious about being proactive will only lead to missed opportunities. If there is a career that interests you but also intimidates you, then don't be afraid to go back to school and learn more. This will be an investment that will do wonders for your career.

Be More Open

If your parents or other family members are urging you to consider a career, be more open to those possibilities. Teenagers often prefer to rebel against their parents and do the complete opposite of what is suggested. However, our loved ones sometimes know things about other professions that we don't. It is advisable to be open about those suggestions, learn about the careers being suggested to you, and find out the options available.

Stay True to Your Values

If you prefer staying close to your family then you won't want to opt for a career that requires traveling a lot. Figure out your priorities and determine if they would be affected by the career you are considering. If there is a potential career that won't allow you to live in the way you want to then it is best to check it off the list.

Avoid Settling

If you have been searching for the right career for a long time and are still confused then continue your research. Don't give up and settle for a career that is dissatisfying for you. You may have to push through your existing job for a while before you find the right one. In the meantime, note down the aspects of your existing career that you like and enjoy doing. Try switching to positions that enable you to do those enjoyable tasks more or where you may learn new skills that may be beneficial for a new job. Don't lose hope, you are bound to find the right career at some point.

Switch Careers

If you have finally found something that you want to do then don't hesitate to change your career. It is normal to have more than one career in your lifetime. You can even become an entrepreneur and create your own independent career out of your past experience, education, and your hobby.

Throughout the 20th century, having a diploma was more than enough to assure employers that an individual can handle the majority of the tasks required for the job. Most of the major organizations had their own internal development and training programs to mold the recent recruits the way they wanted to. These were the reasons most of the Americans enjoyed successful and enjoyable careers and worked at the same company throughout their life. However, the many changes in the global job market for the past few years has put a stop to those traditions. There are very few people who experience the stability of working for one or two companies throughout their life. Since workers now tend to switch more frequently, employers avoid investing in employee training and development programs. Instead they rely on job seekers to develop their own skills before applying. This is the reason why demand for proper educational degrees and additional diplomas and training has drastically increased. This means that it is best that you attend a training session, or attend a workshop or advanced class to develop additional skills.

This is especially true if you are looking for specific career opportunities because entry level requirements have become more complex than ever before. Most of the technical and trade fields require potential employees to get an associate degree before they apply for a position. These degree programs enable job seekers to develop critical skills that are essential for the job. There are some jobs in which it is essential to interact with clients and customers. Such job positions require a bachelor's degree and good communication skills. A bachelor's degree student is more apt to perform tasks properly and has better knowledge to interact with customers effectively.

Another beneficial thing you could do, which thankfully I did, is get some work experience, especially if you aren't able to afford a full time bachelor program or if you are switching careers and don't have the appropriate degree for the particular job you are interested in. I worked as an outpatient rehabilitation clinic office manager while at the same worked on my undergraduate studies. This was one of the best jobs I had. It was great working with the elderly, who tended to appreciate the littlest help, like helping them come through door with their walker, wheelchair, or cane. I went home satisfied on most days after working there. I felt like I accomplished something each day. Such work experience will compensate for whatever you lack in educational qualifications. There are many companies that hire new graduates as interns or give them summer jobs. This is a great way of getting some work experience in the field of your choice. Even if you have the right educational qualifications, I would still suggest you to get some work experience as this will enhance your chances of getting the job you want.

There are plenty of ways through which you can get some work experience. It doesn't necessarily mean that you have to get an internship or summer job at a large company. You can work part-time or intern at your university campus. There were many such opportunities offered to us in my university. Our counselors and teachers used to encourage us to do an internship or get a summer job in order to understand what we learned in the classes and to get a better idea about what a professional life actually is. There are more options for students now than there were back then. You can work as an assistant teacher in your related field, or work in the advertising and publicity offices in your institute to gain practical knowledge that will not only benefit your education but will also enhance your chances of getting your dream job. Each placement provides different benefits and assist the students in establishing better reputations for achieving success early in their professional life.

If you have already entered your professional life and want to enhance your skills and knowledge, there are plenty of adult learning programs that you can benefit from. Today's job market rewards the individuals who can show the abilities and skills of working independently and are able to manage their time effectively. There are plenty of online, evening or weekend courses that you can take advantage of while doing your job. This will show the employers that you are capable enough to manage your time well and have the yearning to learn more.

I assure you there is an abundance of opportunities out there to develop yourself more and learn new skills. Don't be afraid to make mistakes and take chances, this is exactly how we all learn and grow, while taking a step closer to our right career choice and realizing our dreams.

CHAPTER 4

Identifying Your Path and Securing the Right Job

Mornings were chilly in the village, and there was no hot running water available. Nevertheless, I washed outdoors with water fetched from a nearby stream, taking advantage of the morning fog to shield me from view of the neighbors. After that I combed my hair with a wooden comb and slipped on a hand-me-down T-shirt and a pair of shorts made from old bed sheets. Breakfast was usually leftovers kept in clay pots covered to keep out rats and rabbits. The pots this morning contained sweet potatoes and a sorghum drink called obushera. I ate and drank what little remained.

Some family members kept modest parcels of farmland they cultivated for each season's crops. I jogged up the hillside to the vegetable patch, exploiting a route that provided me cover from one of my relatives who had a foul mouth and a short temper. This aunt often cursed violently at my mother, who never responded in kind no matter how severe the assault. If I ever bumped into her, I was advised to be tolerant towards her and win her over with kindness and affection. Today, this aunt was nowhere in view, so I sprang back onto the well-trodden path and continued up the hill. I found my sister and other relatives at the plot digging and singing hymns in our native tongue of Rukiga. I waved and began digging. My sister waved back and pushed onward, never one to waste a moment of daylight.

As I hammered my hoe into the red soil, my mind drifted into dreams of yearning for a better way of life. Living here was simple, but difficult. Jobs were scarce, and most people eked out a meager livelihood by growing and selling crops, or operating small supply stores or vegetable stands. Many shared what little they had with those who had less. Others were blessed to have relatives abroad who sent money for their subsistence. Day laborers sought to carry out what little physical work was available. I observed people bartering and trading goods and services, drawing on creativity and tradition to evaluate one object against another.

After several hours of digging in the sweltering sun, I stopped to gaze around and stretch my back. Surrounding me lay rolling hills terraced with sorghum, millet, cabbage, bananas, or carrots. Out in the distance, cousins and aunties gathered at a relatives' field to lend a hand with planting vegetables for sale and consumption. Small houses constructed from mud with rooftops thatched with grass dotted the foothills as far in each direction as I could observe. Our home was one of the few with a metal roof, which produced harmonious sounds each time it rained.

I dug until a little past midday. Thunder was beginning to rumble in the distance and I knew the rain would be upon us soon. Storms developed rapidly around these parts. Once the showers began, dirt trails would transform into streams of sludge and walking around would be impossible. I rushed down the hillside and headed for cover. The storm barreled through, howling and spitting, then slipped away as rapidly as it had appeared. Villagers emerged from their shelters and went back to whatever chores had been held up by the rain. As fortune would have it, a vendor in whose space I had sought shelter needed someone to help him dig a shallow pit adjacent to his establishment. Digging for a couple of hours netted me five-hundred Ugandan shillings in return, the equivalent of less than one United States dollar yet sufficient to pay for a small meal.

Several years later I was in America. Luckily for me, I had a strong work ethic from growing up in a place of such extreme poverty and hardship. The first job I had immediately upon arrival was cleaning the church my uncle worked in as an administrator. From that church I moved on to became a professional cleaner at a nationwide company, and then a clerk in a clothing store, followed by a certified nursing assistant, an office manager, a Military Police officer (MP) in the United States Army, a clinical data manager, and finally a branch of clinical data management at my current job.

I learned everything by struggling a lot, and would not have made it this far without the guidance of my teachers, friends, colleagues, and relatives. Taking that into consideration I would like to share with you the different ways I relied on to explore my career opportunities.

This Chapter's Takeaways

• Start by focusing on the things you love doing. Make a list of passions you have or what you dreamed of doing in your past. Think of the things that you naturally enjoy doing. Note down everything, no matter how stupid or impossible you think they seem.

- Be on a look out for clues. Jot down the topics or projects that stir your passions or excite you. Think of the people you truly admire and note down what they do for a living. Pay attention to the activities or tasks you enjoy doing. Ask yourself why those activities and tasks make you happy.
- Be patient. It is essential that you understand that this quest for the right career will take some time and you may have to go down several different paths before you end up finding the right career. Introspection and time will assist you in identifying the things that you find satisfying and enjoyable.

I remember the moment I finally decided what I was interested in doing as a career. Even though it felt right, I was stumped about how to proceed and whether it was the right career choice for me. I once again sought the help of my family members and friends. They helped me come up with different ways to analyze the issue. If you find yourself in this position, you too might be wondering how to translate ideas into a career? You will need to do a little research, just like I did. Here are a few ways you can do that.

- Take career tests. There are plenty of online tests and tools available that can help you in this process. Personality assessments, quizzes, and questions will not exactly tell you what would be a perfect career for you but will help you in identifying what you are looking for in a career, your skills, and areas in which you excel. Some tests can also help you in browsing through sample careers on the basis of the personality type you identify most with.

- Conduct research about specific careers. If you have managed to narrow down specific careers or jobs that you may like, find out about them online. From job descriptions to estimated future growth and average salaries; this information will help you in figuring out your practical priorities. Is your field stable? Is there too much risk involved? How much risk are you willing to take? Is the salary range fine for you? What would be the commute distance and costs of travel? Would you have to relocate or train for the career you are considering?
- Get information and support from others. While you can gain a lot of information from career tests and online research, there is no substitute for what you can gain from someone who is already working in the career of your choice. Talking to an individual who is active in your chosen field can help you determine the exact nature of work that you would be doing. This way you can find out whether it would meet your expectations. Best of all, this will help you in building connections in your preferred career which will help you in getting the right job in the future. You can also consider seeking help from a job coach, career counselor, or your family and friends. Impartial advice from professionals and from the ones who know you best can open up even more possibilities that you never considered.

A majority of schools in America have a department that posts job announcements on bulletin boards. These posts can give you more ideas about job qualifications and the responsibilities that each job entails.. These schools also offer career counseling for the students to advise them about their chosen careers or help them decide the right career. The 'Help Wanted' section in the classified ads in newspapers is also a great place to discover different careers and jobs.

Once you have a general idea about your career choice and the career path, you must take some time figuring out the skills required for that career. When I finally decided what career I wanted to go for, I made a list of the skills I already had and the skills that I would need to develop. I assessed and noted down my strengths and weaknesses. I was surprised to realize that there were transferable skills which can be applied to any field. Here are some examples of such skills:

- Fluency in a foreign language
- Computer literacy
- Effective time management
- Mediation and conflict resolution
- Public speaking
- Program and research planning
- Leadership and management experience
- Communication (both oral and written)

If the career you have selected requires experience and skills that you don't have, do not despair. There are numerous ways to develop those skills and gain experience.

Here are a few ways of gaining skills for your chosen career:

- Benefit from your existing position. There are many employers who are willing to pay for their employee's tuition costs if they feel this will benefit their company in the future.
- Identify the sources and resources available to you in your community. There are many productive programs that are offered in different communities. The community libraries and colleges offer reasonably priced oppor-

tunities that enable individuals to develop and strengthen skills like basic accounting, computer courses, language courses, and much more. State job development programs, small business administrations, and local chamber of commerce are also ideal resources.

• Intern or volunteer. There are many career skills that can be developed during an internship or through volunteering. This provides an added advantage of connecting you with individuals in your chosen field and opening up opportunities for your future.

• Take classes. There are many fields that require certain job related skills or education like a specific training or educational degree. You can opt for part-time schooling, or night classes while you continue working. This will help you in developing and expanding your skills and provide you an educational experience that will help your career growth.

These are some valuable steps that will help anyone in finding the right career. Like everyone else, I too struggled to find the career that was right for me. However, these steps helped me figure out my passions and interests and helped me in determining what I really wanted to do in my life. There are so many more resources that can help you in finding the right career, no matter where you are. Don't be afraid to seek help and be creative and you will reap the benefits of having a career you love.

CHAPTER 5

Building and Preserving Fruitful Relationships

By now, news had circulated around the Kigezi High School campus in Western Uganda about me leaving for America, and a large crowd had gathered for a grand send-off. A few teary schoolmates implored me to stay while others rattled off lists of goodies I should send once I settled.

"Don't forget who you are and where you came from," advised one of my classmates.

"I won't," I assured him.

At that moment an old orange-and-white bus rumbled up and my sister and I got on, waving like celebrities to the assembled throng. Just before the doors closed, some of my best friends jumped on board along with my uncle and asked the driver if they could ride with us for a few miles before disembarking. The driver declared it was okay and pulled the lumbering beast of a bus forward, kicking up red dust and spewing thick, black smoke from the exhaust pipe to scatter the crowd back into the dorms.

The bus drove around Kabale town for about an hour picking up individuals from various locations. Passengers piled aboard, lugging with them sacks of food, assorted crafts, stuffed suitcases, live chickens, and appliances. Children sat on their parents' laps or squeezed themselves into nooks not safe enough to transport human beings. For many, this was the sole means of transportation to the capital city of Kampala.

My friends and I had a conversation about the things we would miss about each other. Through trying times and extreme poverty, I had made it this far in life with the love and support of family members and friends. God had blessed me with the most loving and hard working mother. She instilled in me good values, which helped me in becoming a better man. Other important people in my life were my aunts and uncles who believed that I was worth something. I remember my mother not having enough money to pay for my school tuition, books, clothes, and more, but one of my aunts used to take care of all my mom's bills to ease the financial burden. My grandfather and uncles ensured I had a father figure to look up to for manly guidance, especially on how to become a man who positively contributes to the society, among other values. I wasn't one to shed tears, but could sense emotions swelling up inside from the thought of all these relationships about to be severed.

Passengers continued to file into the bus. The temperature was high, and the body odor strong. Most people in the village lacked running water and therefore washed barely once a week. Water was fetched from a borehole or nearby stream and would be used for cooking and doing dishes over bathing. I pulled my shirt over my nose to stop from gagging. Once the bus was full, the driver turned around and directed all my friends to disembark. After a few last hugs and hand slaps, they hopped off and hurried across the road to catch a returning ride. The bus continued down the highway on its way out of Kabale town. In a short while, we approached my home village of Kyobugombe. Normally the bus would pass through to pick up more riders, but since there was no space available, we roared by without stopping. I took one last look at my village, threw open the window, and waved farewell to the place of my birth.

Two years later I was living in America. Shy and soft-spoken, it was a struggle for me to make friends and build relationships outside of family circles. I frequently stayed home when I wasn't working, and today was no exception. Harking back to my earlier years in Uganda, the future didn't look promising unless I made an effort to venture out and build relationships. That would have to wait until the weather improved. Bored and snowbound, I decided to look through some photo albums kept on the living room table.

While going through an old family album, I came across a picture that caught my eye in a way I have never felt in my entire life. I immediately started looking at several other pictures, but I wasn't able to shut my mind from thinking about the beauty I saw in that particular picture. It was a photo of the most beautiful woman I had ever seen in my life. I found myself flipping back to this picture over and over again! This went on for days and days. I asked one of my relatives about her and found out who she was and where she lived. I kept thinking about her for days and made a decision to meet that beautiful woman no matter what it took.

My relative had only told me which neighborhood she lived in, so I used to drive around that neighborhood whenever possible in hopes of seeing her one day. I kept praying to God that I could at least catch a glimpse of her in real life, but no such luck. However, God's works in mysterious ways. I was invited to a Christmas Eve party by a family friend. I went to the party in high spirits as I always loved Christmas parties. I stood near the door chatting with a few friends when guess who arrived at the party? That gorgeous woman whom I couldn't get out of my mind! I couldn't believe my eyes ... the woman I was going crazy for was standing a few steps away from me! She was even more beautiful than she was in the photo. The minute I gathered up my courage to introduce myself and started talking with her, I knew she was the one.

Our relationship blossomed from there. She became my best friend, my supporter, and the reason for me to become an even better version of myself. To this day, she still teases me about how I unsuccessfully tried to stalk her. I later found out that she had no plans of coming to that party but only came due to the insistence of her mother. It truly was a blessing from God that she came to that party that evening. This amazing blessing gave me two handsome sons, who make me feel so proud every day.

Meeting the right friends and colleagues, has also been a blessing as well. I have had great friends and still have pretty amazing friends who have made a great impact on my life. I have friends who support me and colleagues who give me genuine advice whenever I need it. My flower introduced me to my first ice cream ever. On our first date, I didn't have any money on me so she ordered one cup of ice cream and we sat in one of the smallest ice cream shops you can find in Maryland. Though I was not sure what I was getting myself into being a very picky shy guy who had never tasted ice cream before, I was ready to impress by digging into that small ice cream cup. It turned out to be the best ice cream I had ever tasted. Regardless of this great experience though, I have not gotten myself to enjoy it after that. When you see me enjoying a DQ short cake ice cream, just keep in mind I am doing it to take one for the team.

The support and love of my loving family has made a huge impact on my life. Not just my family, but I have always been lucky to be blessed with supporting teachers, mentors, friends, and colleagues. They all have helped me in each aspect of my life, guiding me towards the right path and helping me make the right decisions. All the things I have earned and achieved are because of the help and support of the people around me. This has confirmed my belief in how the people we are around all the time can shape up our lives, either for the better or for the worst.

This Chapter's Takeaways

Building and preserving fruitful relationships is very important if you wish to make any headway in achieving the American dream. It's impossible to do everything by yourself, so knowing how to build relationships will enlarge your network of people that can help you in times of need. There is an art to this, so let's discuss some of the relationship building techniques now.

Identify people who have similar goals and values. There is no sense building relationships with someone diametrically opposed to your world view or sense of values or ethics. While it's important to respect a diversity of opinions or even learn from people with different views, maintaining your moral compass is something you will need to do even while building your network. The quality of your relationships is more important than the quantity.

Be proactive. Don't wait for people to discover you, or else you might end up waiting forever. When you encounter somebody you consider worthy of building a relationship with, introduce yourself in the appropriate manner and slowly begin the process.

Be authentic and transparent. This helps you attract the kind of people who share similar views. If you pretend to be something you're not in order to attract people, you will end up building relationships that will be of no benefit to either side based on a phony personality. It's okay to have some secrets or things you can't share openly with everyone, but some level of transparency is required in order for you to display your authentic self.

Be reliable and dependable. This is one of the best ways to build lasting relationships with people who can assist you in your endeavors. When somebody can take you at your word and be sure that you will come through when you say you will, they in turn will be there for you when you need them.

Show an interest in people. Don't make everything about you all the time. If people think you only care about yourself and your needs, they won't be interested in developing a relationship with you. Show concern for other people, be willing to discuss things they are interested in, ask them questions about themselves, and care about their well being.

Show appreciation. Nobody likes someone who never says "Thank you" or acknowledges when somebody does something nice. Be the kind of person who shows humility and appreciation, and you will be able to build a larger network of friends.

Network. Be flexible and open-minded about the places where you can network. You don't have to wait for specially scheduled networking events to do your networking. Birthday parties, picnics, fundraisers, barbecue events, games, conferences, seminars, the grocery store; many locations can serve as a place for you to meet people with shared values to network with.

Help, share, or give before asking for something. The most effective relationship building technique is to be helpful to others before asking them to help you. Offer advice, help, experience, or resources to others and they will be willing to give you something in return.

Build a relationship over time. Nobody is going to jump into a massive project with or have complete faith in a complete stranger. Start small, with for example organizing a birthday party, and then work up to doing bigger and more complex things with members of your network. Eventually you will have a strong relationship and be able to trust each other with more important things.

Meet regularly. When you meet people at regular intervals, it gives you an opportunity to brainstorm and discuss ideas. This is not only helpful from the standpoint of solving problems and coming up with solutions to challenges, but also of deepening your relationships.

Stay in touch. In addition to meeting regularly, it is important to stay in touch with the people in your network. We often get busy or move to other locations and sometimes lose touch with people in our contact list. If you don't stay in touch you eventually fall off each other's radar, removing a link from the chain of people who can be of help to you at some point in your life.

Be honest and trustworthy. If people can't trust you, they won't want to build a relationship with you. Your reputation travels, so being known as a trustworthy and honest person will expand your network. You can be trustworthy with information, property, funds, relationships, and so on.

Make your friends look good. When somebody from within your network refers you to someone or vice versa, don't let them down by not acting appropriately or coming through for them. Be somebody that other people want to have in their circle.

Be tactful. Choose your words carefully. Words have meaning and are very powerful, so don't be careless with your choice of words when talking to or about people. Saying the wrong thing can jeopardize relationships at home, within family circles, at the workplace, or among your network of friends.

Maintain standards, but don't be too judgmental. Nobody is perfect, yourself included. Keep an open mind and get to know people before you fully accept them or write them off.

Don't hold things too close to your chest. If you appear too secretive, you will give off the impression that you are "shady" or have something to hide. It's okay to be discrete (particularly with information you shouldn't be sharing), but being too tight-lipped can turn people off and make them not want to build a relationship with you.

Be nice to be around. If nobody likes being around you, you will have a hard time building and preserving relationships that are fruitful and long lasting.

So, why is it important for you to bother building and preserving relationships?

People can offer you useful advice or help you find lasting solutions to some of the problems you may be facing.

People within your network can help you get things done that you might not be able to do yourself, like make a phone call, arrange a meeting, book an interview, reach a contact, create an opportunity, etc.

Especially in the early months and years of your arrival to the United States, people can offer you a place to stay while you're working on getting your education or finding a way to earn a salary.

If you're looking for a job, people who you have relationships with might offer a lead to a job opening or put in a good work at their place of employment for you.

Relationships can be a source of lending or borrowing in times of need.

Your network can be a place where you can solicit references for particular applications (employment, visa, passport, rental, etc).

Your network can be a place to find customers or get referrals from if you run a business. In addition, you can also find potential business partners from within your network of friends.

You can get investment ideas or discover other money making opportunities from within your network.

You can get updates or confirm important news items from members of your network who share similar values and are concerned about the same things. This is particularly useful in immigrant communities where information about visas and related rules and regulations change constantly.

You can get introduced to new people from other people within your network, thus expanding the circle even further than you would be able to on your own. Sometimes the best way to be introduced to somebody is from someone else within your network.

People within your network can become allies and help spread the word about your business, cause, or issue of interest. These "evangelists" can be more effective as a marketing campaign than paid advertising.

Whether we need a motivational boost, a shoulder to cry on, mentorship, a lead on a new job, clarity in our goals, if we have the right people in our life, then nothing remains difficult. Meeting the right people usually requires establishing links with those who can assist us with something, in other words, successful networking. Sounds easy? It actually is rather tricky in practice. Let me help you out a little. Here are a few tips you can try out:

Defining your needs.

Let's assume that your computer has suddenly crashed and needs immediate IT assistance. In this scenario, your colleagues might offer support by listening to you rant about how unlucky it is that your system crashed, how much time you would lose, and the list of methodologies you think would help you deal with this situation. However, the 'right' individual would be the one who could get your computer running again and help you learn how to avoid such a scenario in future. You already have an idea who the right person would be to help you out in this situation since you have a specific and clear need.

The same applies when it comes to meeting the right people in other contexts. When you have a clear idea about what you want or need then meeting people who would help you out can become a lot easier. Start by asking yourself what kind of people you want in your life. Why do you want to meet new people? You will immediately get some general ideas about the type of friends you want for yourself. You will also get some ideas about where you can find such individuals. This will help you in including the right people in your life.

Effectively engaging with people around you.

Having a clear idea about your needs and wants from the people around you is essential, but developing a proactive approach towards meeting people is also important. A majority of individuals think that this means attending conferences or seminars and approaching an individual they don't know, which can be very intimidating. However, this isn't the case. You can start small by enhancing your networking skills through engaging with people who work around you. People whom you see every day at work but rarely talk to. Instead of a simple 'hello' or 'morning', try asking them how their work is going, or comment about a recent happening at work or in the town. Getting to know your colleagues is a great way of improving your networking skills.

Moreover, try engaging in more meaningful conversations with them. You will find that your colleagues will willingly offer valuable advice and offer support to you. This is a good way of building stronger relationships. As your networking skills start improving, you will gain the confidence needed to spark a conversation with people you don't know. This will help you in getting to know others well and will enable you to spend more time with the ones you want to be a part of your life.

Assuming people will help you and giving them a chance to do it.

To be honest, there is no 'right' person to meet. Each person you know or may meet in future will have certain benefits to offer to you, such as useful advice, new opportunities, and so on. Yet no one is perfect. Each of us have some good attributes and some bad ones. Make sure you realize this and start giving others an opportunity to help you out in their own way. Each of us has within ourselves the tendency and desire to help others out, especially when asked to do so. This means that all you have to do is ask for help and people will come to your aid.

If you are struggling and require help, don't suffer in silence. Tell someone. When stuck with a complex task at work, for example, ask for help. Doing so could lead to a helpful solution, a great friendship, a new lead, a strong contact or a load of other ideas. We rarely give people the chance to help us out. We make assumptions that there won't be anyone to help us or rely on. This closes off any possible opportunities that could come our way. Only when you start to eliminate these unhelpful assumptions will networking become effortless for you and the right people will start coming in your life.

Making an effort to help others.

Meeting the right people is a two way process. You must be willing to give what you expect in return. Always be open to help other people out as well. The more you do for others, the more others will do for you. By helping out others and engaging with them, you will be able to create opportunities for yourself to offer advice, lend a sympathetic ear, or share your perspective. This will help you in feeling confident to reach out to others. Helping others will also make you feel better about yourself.

These are a few tips that I know could help you in attracting positive people in your life. Remember that people are walking opportunities, and many of them are also interesting individuals. You will learn so much from their experiences, their struggles, their dreams, and their aspirations. This will help you grow your perspective about this world and also give you ideas about how to manage your life in a better way. I know this because I have many friends and mentors I have learned a lot from.

CHAPTER 6

Purchasing a Home

After a longer than anticipated ride, we arrived at the edge of Kabale town in Western Uganda late at night sore and exhausted. The sole light for miles came from the old bus' dim headlamps. I pulled out a flashlight and tested it to make sure the batteries worked, then my sister and I split up from our uncle and walked the quarter of a mile to our village. We entered the house and I tiptoed into one of the bedrooms, feeling along the floor in search of a space with a straw mat. Nudging past cousins curled in slumber, I slid under the worn blanket and was sound asleep within minutes.

We were poor, yet no child went without a place to call home. There was always somewhere you could stay whether or not you were a direct family member or had a title to the property. In that sense homes, even though modest, were important as an anchor in the community. Since large families living together in one home was the norm in Uganda, especially in the villages, I had grown up with a strong sense of community. I remember as a child growing up how my friends and I had sleep-overs all of the time. I grew up witnessing family members and other villagers helping one another, supporting each other in times of need, and rejoicing in each other's success. We had very little in terms of physical possessions and income, but a home was always something that was available.

Several years later I arrived in the United States on a cold winter's day in February. I distinctly remember the first experience I had living in a proper house. Leaving Dulles airport in the state of Virginia, we rode along the highway for what seemed like an hour before entering Washington D.C., the capital of the United States. In contrast to the streets of Kampala, everything here appeared organized and clean. The sidewalks were free of vendors and clutter. Pedestrians appeared to be going to or from some place with a purpose, and not milling about aimlessly. Mannequins in department store windows leaned and posed with confidence. Streetlights illuminated the network of roads extending north, south, east, and west.

Melted balls of ice splattered against the windshield as we continued out of the capital and into the suburbs of Maryland. We arrived at the house my mother shared with her sister and brother-in-law late into the evening. My uncle parked the car a short distance ahead and we walked back. Children squealed in delight out in the yard as they threw snowballs at each other, unconcerned about the new guests approaching. We walked up the slippery driveway to the front entrance.

I was reluctant to be the first one to go in, so I pulled my sister from behind me and urged her to enter first. Initially, she resisted as well, but after a little coaxing, acquiesced and pushed the door open. Everyone appeared to have been prepared for our entrance, and upon realizing we had come in, erupted in a chorus of celebration. Most faces were unknown to me and it felt a little weird responding to a room full of strangers. However, I knew these were relatives and friends elated to meet my sister and me, so I shrugged off the thought and pushed myself to embrace the moment.

We made our rounds saying hello to everyone and describing our journey over the last several days. There was so much to talk about and so many people to talk with. I could feel my cheeks hurting from so much grinning and smiling, but also my body ached due to so many hours of sitting on the plane. Everybody wanted to have a conversation with us and catch up, but thoughtfully, my mother stepped in and recommended we have dinner and get some sleep.

We assembled at the dinner table arranged with an assortment of foods that I was used to eating along with some new dishes. I interpreted this as an effort to ease my transition to a different cuisine. A family friend said a quick prayer, followed by a brief speech by my uncle, after which we sat down to dig in. The matooke (bananas prepared while the skin is still green) was not quite the same version I was familiar with, but I appreciated the effort, nonetheless. During dinner, I found myself asking more questions of them than they were asking of me. We talked and ate for over two hours, by which time I began to feel the effects of fatigue from the long flight. I asked to be excused from the table and went with my mother to a room upstairs where I would be staying.

We conversed together for a few minutes before bidding each other goodnight. I lay alone in the room lit by a small table lamp and drew in a huge sigh of contentment. The mattress felt extremely comfortable compared to the rug I was accustomed to sleeping on. The fluffy pillow embraced my head in support and the sheets felt soft to the touch. My first day in America was ending. Tomorrow would be a new day and the beginning of my new life. I curled myself into a ball and slid off into a sweet slumber.

I lived in that house for several years while going to school, and once I got settled I found it important to look into purchasing a house both as an asset and an anchor. After all, to many, owning a home was part of the American Dream. I moved out of the spare room and into an apartment, then to my first house, and finally to the house I now own and occupy with my beautiful wife and two wonderful sons.

This Chapter's Takeaway

I learned lessons and took some bumps along the way, and following are some tips to help you avoid some common mistakes and make your purchase the right way.

Live in an apartment for a couple of years to get into the habit of making monthly payments consistently. You will also utilize this time to familiarize yourself with how much earning potential you have and what amount of monthly payments you can afford to make without straining yourself.

Don't waste too much time trying to figure out the best time to purchase a home. Nobody has a crystal ball that enables them to see into the future. How owning a home fits into your long-term plans along with whether you can afford to make the mortgage payments are the most important things to consider. You will notice the market fluctuate and interest rates rise and fall, but no matter when you buy, you will always feel like there might have been a better time to jump in. Therefore, determine that a home fits into your plans, find the house you want and can afford, and go for it.

Make sure you have a consistent source of income and a long-term plan for maintaining or even increasing the amount you earn. A home purchase is a long-term commitment, and relying on the idea that the home will always appreciate in value and be easy to sell in a crunch is not a good idea to rely on. Look at the purchase from the perspective that you may have to be responsible for the mortgage for the entire duration of the contract. If that idea makes you uncomfortable, then hold off on the purchase until you are ready to make the commitment.

Work diligently on increasing your credit score to ensure that it is good or excellent by the time you're ready to buy a home. Start by getting a secured credit card and only utilizing 30% of the available credit while making more than the minimum monthly payment. Keep this up for several months and it will begin your positive credit history. Continue with perhaps a department store card or a vehicle loan. Having good credit will come to your benefit when you begin the process of getting a mortgage loan.

Know what lenders care about. Unless you have a bucket load of cash lying around, you're most likely going to need to apply for a loan to purchase your home. If that's the case, it pays to know what lenders look for. The basic things that lenders look for are the amount of debt you're carrying, your monthly income, and the length of your employment. If any of these raise a flag, your chances of getting a loan diminish. Make sure that before you apply, your level of debt is low (relative to your income), your monthly income is as high as possible, and you've been at your current job for a long time.

Avoid making large purchases, moving your money around, or opening any new credit accounts up to a year before applying for a mortgage loan in order to avoid a dip in your credit score. Lenders will be looking at your financial stability and the level of activity of your accounts in order to decide whether to risk giving you a loan. Taking on too much debt leading up to your application will make them unsure about your ability to handle an increase in payments.

Open up a savings account and ensure there is a decent amount of money in there. When it comes to applying for a home loan, any potential lender would want to know that you're not living from paycheck to paycheck. Showing that you have a savings culture and a backup funding source gives the lender confidence that you will not default on the loan. Even having five or six months of your mortgage payments available can make the difference in your chances of getting your loan approved.

Start putting money aside for your home early. This will ensure you have a decent amount of money available for your down payment, closing costs, and costs associated with moving in to your new home (furnishing, appliances, renovations, etc). In a crunch, you can take advantage of first-time home buyer programs to help with your down payment. Owning a home comes with many costs that are often out of view in the romance of the chase, including insurance, property taxes, repairs, maintenance costs, utilities, association dues, and more. These costs can creep up on you, and if you're caught unaware and start to fall behind, it can be a nightmare trying to keep up with all the payments.

Research your mortgage options and consider the impact of various mortgage rates on your finances. Your income and budget should help you determine what's best, but you should not wait until the last minute or fail to consider all options before starting to look at homes and making offers. If you wait until too late you will make a decision based not on best financial practices, but desperation and an excitement to move into your new home.

Decide, and be very clear about, exactly how much home you can afford. This means not just knowing how much of a monthly mortgage you can afford to pay (the principal and interest), but also what the costs of property taxes, homeowner's insurance, association fees, utilities, etc, are. It's quite easy to underestimate your payments and accept more of a loan than you can afford to pay off.

Get a loan pre-approval before looking at homes. Having a loan pre-approved not only assures the seller you can afford the home, but also gives you an idea of the range of homes to look at. As a benefit of joining the army I was able to take advantage of the VA loan privilege on my second home that covered moving costs and required no money down. This gave the seller confidence that the deal would go through once I made an offer.

Once you're ready to buy your home, employ the expertise of a buyer's agent. My wife and I used an agent when we purchased our first home and the advice and time-savings we were provided with proved indispensable. Besides access to information about homes on the market, the agent helped us pick the most comfortable neighborhood and understand exactly how much we could afford to pay for the house. Keep in mind, however, that your agent will be working on a commission basis, therefore some of their choices may be made in their best financial interest and not yours. Use your head even while you avail yourself of their advice and expertise.

Print out a bunch of checklists to take with you when you go looking for homes. Include on the checklists all the things that are "must-haves", "nice-to-haves", and "optional". As you go around each home, check off each item that happens to be on the list. This will help you keep your eye on the items you really desired, and prevent you from selecting a home with nothing from the list which, even if nice now at the height of the romance, will turn out to disappoint you at some point down the road.

As you look around, don't fall in love with a home you can't afford. Stay under your pre-approval limit and avoid getting into bidding wars with other buyers. Keep your emotions out of the process. Almost all the homes we saw that we liked initially would have been a stretch to maintain monthly payments on. We found it tempting to strain ourselves financially in order to get into a beautiful home in hopes that money would magically materialize later. Ultimately, we decided to purchase an affordable first home within our means and then upgrade later.

Beware of staging. When looking at homes, pay attention to the layout of the home as opposed to how great all the furniture looks inside the house. A great deal of effort has been applied in "staging" the home with furniture and appliances to look fabulous, including positioning items in ways that are not even be possible for you to accomplish if you buy the home. Purchase the home for the layout and the items on your checklist, and then conduct your own interior decorating once you've moved in.

If you find a home you're interested in purchasing, inquire about whether it is part of a home owner's association. If so, ask to take a look at the contract. You may discover things in the contract that conflict with your long-term goals of owning a home in that area. Better to find those things out before purchasing the home.

Before you make an offer on a home, spend a little bit of time walking (or driving) around to get a sense of the neighborhood. Pay attention to not only the other homes in the vicinity, but also the comings and goings of neighbors and traffic. Notice what kinds of activities take place and what types of people visit. See if there are any parks, schools, retail or business establishments, and more within short distance of the home. Consider how your daily commute will be from the home you're considering purchasing to your place of work. Take into account anything that might impact your lifestyle and way of life.

Select a home that fits well among the rest of the homes in the neighborhood. Avoid purchasing the largest home in the area because it will be the outlier and may be difficult to sell if you ever are in the position to need to do so. Your profit margin will be the same no matter which home you pick, but your ability to find willing buyers will be hampered by the outsize sticker price of your larger home. Besides, the largest home will make a bigger target for home invasions. Our current home is about average for the area, not the largest or the smallest, and serves our needs nicely.

Conduct a home inspection before making an offer on the house you're interested in. Whatever things you discover at this stage will not only help with the price you end up negotiating but also will reveal potential problems that could make the house not worth buying. No matter how closely you look at a house, there are always hidden things that only a trained, licensed inspector will be able to find. The costs of the inspection will dwarf any unseen disasters waiting to land on your lap from leaking roofs, rotting decks, cracked foundation, moldy drywall, failing A/C units, and more.

In addition to a home inspection, conduct a site survey of the property in question to determine exactly where the borders lie. This will help you avoid any disputes with your neighbors as well as enable you to access the property value more accurately. Luckily for us, our first purchase was a townhouse which had clearly delineated property lines for each house, making any disputes about boundaries entirely unnecessary.

Negotiate the offer from the seller. Most people think the price of a home is determined by market value, recent sales, and so on, but the fact is that the seller can ask for whatever price they want. This means if you don't negotiate you may end up paying more for the house than is necessary. Make your bid reasonable and fair according to what other homes in the area have sold for, and consider what you can afford. Don't make a bid that is so low as to offend the homeowner, yet avoid getting dragged into a bidding war.

Once you've bought your home, it is very important to start building an emergency fund for unexpected expenses. Even with a new home, the earlier you begin this process, the better off you will be when something arises a couple of years into owning your home.

Perform maintenance to your home in order to minimize the scope of damage that can arise from neglecting repairs. Regular maintenance will enable you to tackle problems when they are still manageable (like for example repairing or replacing individual parts) rather than waiting until an entire unit needs to be replaced.

Don't expect to get rich from selling your home. Continue to put money into a savings scheme to fund your retirement. If you sell your home (and if you can continue earning some income), you can use the money that was paying your monthly mortgage to fund some of your retirement.

These are some of the tips I have for you as you consider purchasing a home. As I mentioned earlier, home ownership, to some, is one important aspect of living the American dream, and I hope the tips in this chapter can help you make your dream a reality.

CHAPTER 7

Establishing and Running a Successful Business

The warm tropical breeze rushed through the open car windows while a mix of Lingala and reggae tunes blared from a tiny handheld radio. We drove through the busy Kampala streets past buyers and vendors haggling for advantage outside stores splashed with drink and detergent logos. Motorcyclists negotiated with riders for cheap fares to their destinations while taxi drivers looked on with envy. Women stocked their vegetable stands with produce while men hacked away at fresh meat along roadside butcheries.

Within a half hour, we were by the shores of Lake Victoria approaching the airport. Heads of swimmers bobbed in the swell close to shore while in the distance fishermen spread their nets in hope of a big days catch. Traffic slowed to weave past spikes set up at a makeshift checkpoint where truck drivers slipped jugs of milk and assorted goodies to the police officers to enable hassle-free passage. As we drove up, an officer peered into the car then nodded and waved us through. It didn't appear to him we were worth the hassle. Ahead of us trucks loaded with timber plied the single-lane highway along with buses ferrying passengers upcountry.

By all the activity around, it was plainly clear that Ugandans were very much entrepreneurs in nature and culture. The problem of extreme poverty that most people endured was a result of the low cost, low profit, low income model of doing business, and this I could clearly see. Nevertheless, I always thought I had it within myself to one day start a business of my own.

We continued along the single lane highway, which opened to three lanes as we turned the bend toward the airport. Looming ahead was the widest set of concrete structures I had ever seen. From my vantage point, the aircraft lined up on the runway looked small, yet impressive. Compared to the small tourist aircraft I had observed flying overhead in my village before, these planes looked extraordinary. They had many more windows on the side, splashes of color on the tails, and sets of enormous engines hanging off the wings. I wanted to get a closer look at them but an imposing security fence sat between the runway and us. Despite my pleas to stop, my cousin kept driving to the departure area of the airport and pulled into a vacant spot in the parking lot. My sister and I stepped out of the car and waited for a few relatives to show up, then we walked the short distance to the main terminal.

"Security is always high at airports," my uncle explained. "A daring hostage rescue operation by Israeli commandos took place here in the 1970s. Many people were killed, and several movies were made about this incident," he continued.

"Oh? I never knew about that," I responded.

"You should watch 'The Raid on Entebbe' with Charles Bronson," he suggested. "It depicts the events in explicit detail."

For a moment, the place took on an eerie quality. It was distressing to learn so many lives were lost at the spot where I was taking off to pursue my dreams. I looked around at all the travelers arriving and departing and was grateful that all was calm today. We continued into the terminal and came upon a long line leading up to the British Airways counter. I took this occasion to give final hugs and farewell kisses to all the relatives that had turned up to see me off.

When we reached the head of the line, my sister and I moved forward to the counter with my uncle and handed over our tickets. I learned from the ticket agent that my mother had arranged assistance for us for the whole trip since this was our first time flying. That discovery made me feel more relaxed. Since we had no luggage, the checking in process was brief and pain-free, after which we proceeded toward our gate. As we approached, passengers were already preparing to board the plane, so we hastened our good-byes.

"Thank you uncle Kibuchu for all your support and unselfish care, as well for being such a strong father figure," I uttered. "I will miss you."

"Yes Dixion. I will miss you as well. Remember all that we taught you and try to help others as you have been helped."

With those wise words said we embraced, then separated and continued on our way. My sister and I handed over our boarding passes to the airline employees at the gate as my uncle strode off toward the airport exit.

Suddenly, I caught my first glimpse through the waiting lounge window at Entebbe airport of the aircraft parked on the asphalt and reeled back in disbelief. From this short distance, it now appeared humongous and imposing. The largest vehicle I had seen was a truck carrying timber through my village, and this plane was at least four times the size of that. That anything this large could remain in the sky flabbergasted me. This would be my transport to the United States, and I was eager to get going.

Amused at my naiveté, an airline representative motioned me over and accompanied my sister and I through a doorway that let out onto the asphalt. We walked a short distance to the plane and arrived at the foot of a set of air stairs reaching up to the plane doors. I paused at the bottom of the steps for three or four seconds while gazing back toward the terminal. I had never traveled this far away from my village, and everything I had known lay in the direction I was leaving. A new experience awaited, so I pulled myself upward two steps at a time.

A smiling flight attendant greeted us at the plane doors then welcomed us aboard the aircraft and escorted us to our seats. I sat with my sister beside me and peeked out of the window. Meanwhile, the plane continued to fill with passengers until everybody was accounted for. At that point, the flight attendants secured the doors in preparation for departure.

The idling engines roared to life as the plane advanced away from the terminal. We bumped along on the asphalt leading to the runway while the flight attendants read safety instructions.

"In the event of an emergency, you can use your seat as a flotation device."

My sister and I looked at each other in alarm. Since no one else appeared shaken by the instructions, we considered this normal so we relaxed.

Shortly afterward, we heard the voice of the captain informing us that we stood next in line for takeoff. The flight attendants completed their routine and harnessed themselves into their seats. The plane turned and slowed for a moment, then the engines screamed to full throttle as we surged forward. I felt myself pinned back against the seat as we accelerated down the runway. At the same time, my sister grabbed my hand and shut her eyes. Suddenly the rumble of wheels against asphalt ceased, and a sensation of weightlessness overcame me as the plane lifted off the ground. Up we soared, higher into the sky and farther away from land each second. Into the clouds we ascended, then burst out into glorious sunlight. I finally was on my way and somehow knew my life would be changed forever.

The entrepreneurial flame burned inside me for a long time following my arrival to the United States. After undergoing several years of study and undertaking several jobs at different companies, I finally felt ready to venture out and get into business. The first company I started was a DJ company. I figured I would take my love for music and combine it with passion for running a business. The model would revolve around providing music and master of ceremony (MC) services for weddings, corporate events, and so on. I recruited my brother-in-law, who had spent many years in the music business, to help me launch the idea. Together we came up with a list of equipment to buy from the budget I had put aside from my savings, and got under way. I then registered the business, joined a prominent DJ association, put together a website, printed out promotional materials and business cards, and bought a vehicle. Before long we were in business, and turning a modest profit from doing weekend gigs for a few hundred dollars each.

A few years later, I decided to use my expertise in the clinical data management field to write a series of instructional manuals. I spent a lot of time writing the books and editing the information into actionable intelligence that could be of benefit to those trying to enter the field. Ultimately, this business died off as a result of lack of a sufficient number of buyers. However, the efforts involved in this venture sparked the birth of my next business in the same field. This business is now running successfully and turning a healthy profit.

As a result of running these businesses, I have a wealth of experience I would like to tap into to help you with your dream of establishing and running a successful business of your own.

This Chapter's Takeaways.

Try and combine your passion, skill, talent, expertise, training, or education with a genuine need. Ensure that there is a market for whatever it is you're trying to sell, and the market is large enough for sufficient sales. In the second business I launched, the need for what I was providing was insufficient, and therefore my passion and expertise was irrelevant and the business folded.

Add business experience, apprenticeship, training, or courses to your passion. Just because you have a passion or skill doesn't necessarily mean you have the acumen to run a business successfully. Many of us have a passion or talent for something, but you need to also know how to determine your cost of goods, develop a management and marketing strategy, balance the books, and do a whole host of things in order to run a successful business. Even with outsourcing, you need to have a solid business strategy and develop and maintain the overall direction of the company.

Ensure the business makes sense on paper. While it's fine to go with your gut and instincts, the plan for your business must be viable. Crunch the numbers and evaluate the strategy. If it doesn't make sense on paper, it won't make sense in practice.

Ensure you have the time to actually run the business. In the beginning, you will need to do most of the work of running the business by yourself or with one or two partners. Make sure you have the time to put in the amount of hours required to get your business off the ground and running successfully. Many a business has failed even with a good idea and a market because the owner was unable to put in enough time to fulfill orders and meet demand.

Select a business name and create a logo. Depending on the business type, come up with a name for your business that projects the kind of vibe and image you want your customer to associate with. The same applies to your logo. In some instances, the look of the name and logo of a business has either increased or decreased the chances of a sale in the eyes of a customer.

Decide on your business structure (sole proprietorship, partnership, LLC, corporation, nonprofit.) Depending on the type of business you intend to run and how many employees you intend to hire, conduct research on the various business structures and the tax obligations. Remember that even if your business makes no money or profit, there may be certain taxes (like property taxes) that you might be required to pay regardless.

Get all applicable licenses, permits, and insurance in order. Many small businesses can get under way with just a business name registration, but some businesses also require permits and special insurance to legally operate. Make sure you've researched the regulations covering your particular venture and ensure everything is in order before launching.

Avoid overcrowded markets. Don't launch a business in a saturated market. It will be difficult to stand out and make enough profit to survive. If lots of people are doing something, the share of the overall pie will be smaller for each player. For example, the DJ company I started only made modest profit because the field was saturated. Thankfully, I wasn't relying on it to be my sole source of income at that time. I still, however, do gigs from time to time simply because of my love for music and making people happy.

Stand out. Whatever your business idea is, find a way to differentiate yourself from other businesses. Have a unique selling proposition. This doesn't have to be anything fancy or expensive. Differentiate yourself by adding a twist to the product, providing excellent customer service, having attractive pricing structure, and so on. Find ways to stand out from others in your field.

Try and start your first business using your own money instead of borrowing. Resist borrowing money on your first business venture, even from friends and family members. No matter how confident you are in your skill or your product or service, your first business will involve a lot of trial and error before turning a profit. The last thing you need while trying to run the business is worrying about paying back a loan when you're barely even meeting and paying expenses. Worse, if your business fails, you'll still be stuck having to pay off the loan. If you don't have the money saved or otherwise available from a generous donor, consider holding off on the venture. Depending on the type of business and your background, a loan is best sought when you need to expand operations or add to your line of products, not when you're first starting out.

Don't underestimate the amount of money needed to launch and operate the business. Many people come up with the smallest number they can conjure up in order to convince themselves or investors that the business can launch with little money. You will only be fooling yourself if you attempt this illusion. In fact, whatever the number is that you initially come up with in your estimate; double it. Don't start your business until you have adequate funding to cover your startup and operational expenses.

Reduce your needs to the bare minimum the business requires to operate. Don't overspend by adding things to your wish list that the business doesn't really need in the beginning. It's tempting to want things like fancy office space, company vehicles, large warehouses, and such for your business, but that can quickly eat through your budget and leave you unable to continue operations. Start with what you need, turn a profit, and then add from there.

You will need a much stronger marketing, publicity, and promotional plan than you initially visualize. Getting the word out about your business to reach your prospective clients in a crowded marketplace will require a lot of resources. Don't assume that your product is so amazing that it will simply sell itself. Depending on the type of business you will be operating, you may only convert 1% of the people who hear about your business into paying customers. Whichever marketing methods you employ, the volume of "eyeballs" you reach will need to be extremely high, so you must ensure that the marketing budget you put aside is adequate for your needs.

Have a "rainy day" fund. You will need to be patient with your business. No matter how good your product or service is, it takes time to reach the potential buyers or subscribers, and in the meantime you will need to keep the bills paid. Your profits will take some time to materialize. Having a fund from which you can tap for expenses and emergencies can make the difference between eventual success and a retreat into defeat.

Build your business over time. Don't start with a full menu of products, services, and expenses until you've seen that a few items can turn a profit. While this might not be an issue with digital products or online services, starting out too big in the physical world can result in a business stumbling out of the starting blocks and crumbling under its own weight. Start with whatever is manageable for you, and then build from there.

Establish relationships with mentors or other successful entrepreneurs in your area of interest. Nothing beats experience and success, and since in the early days you will have neither, it will be in your best interest to associate yourself with people that do.

Use your competitors for research. Conduct a search online for businesses similar to yours and look over their offerings, then find ways to offer things they don't. Also, search for customer complaints about businesses in your field, then make efforts to avoid doing those things. In that way, you need not be afraid of your competition since they will be helping you to find your niche.

Establishing and running a successful business is for some people a part of living the American dream, and I hope these tips will aid you in your quest to live yours.

CHAPTER 8

Enlisting and Serving in the US. Military

The idea to enlist in the US Military revolved around my urge to give back to a country that had given me so many blessings and helped me live the life I always wanted. Around the time I was contemplating the proposition, I knew that most people harbored fears about their loved ones joining the military. My wife, my Flower, was one of them. Even as I thought of other ways to give back, the option of joining the army kept rising to the top of the list. Eventually I gathered the courage to broach the topic with her, and a long series of conversations ensued. Finally, after much counseling, I was able to convince her that it would be good for the family and she agreed. This came as a relief to me since by that point I had become very interested in enlisting. The next task was to convince the rest of my family.

Serving the US military is indeed one of the greatest honors of my life. There are many people who have this urge to serve and protect their country. While serving, I had the privilege of traveling to places in and out of the country on multiple occasions. Some of the places included Mali, Kuwait, Iraq, Uganda, as well as different states within the U.S.A. My missions included training as well as combat. The US. military comprise of the most respected and dedicated soldiers in the world. These soldiers protect the freedom of America and protect its people by serving at the home front or abroad. They are always ready to defend their country from any threat that comes its way. The US military is the true essence of mental and physical strength. Being a soldier means you should be prepared to serve wherever and whenever there is a need. It means living up to a high standard.

Serving the military taught me the real meaning of a disciplined life, the essence of loyalty, honor, and respect. I have started living up to their true meanings which has changed my life for the better. Soldiers learn these values during their training and start living their lives incorporating these values, even when they are off the job.

This Chapter's Takeaways

The most essential core values I learned are:

Loyalty

Soldiers learn to bear true allegiance and faith to the American constitution, the entire team, and other soldiers. Bearing true allegiance and faith means truly believing and dedicating yourself to the country. Being a loyal soldier means you support your leader and stand up for your fellow soldiers. Wearing the US. military uniform means being loyal to the country, to its beliefs, and to the unit.

Duty

US military soldiers always fulfill their obligations. Performing your duty means doing more than simply doing the assigned tasks. It means accomplishing tasks as a team.

The work of a soldier is challenging and complex with a mixture of responsibilities and tasks constantly in motion. It means staying true to your values while performing your tasks and resisting the urge to take 'shortcuts' that can jeopardize the country's integrity.

Respect

As a soldier, it is your responsibility to respect others. It is essential to treat others with dignity and expect others to do the same, even when you are off duty. This trait enables one to appreciate the best in others. Respect means trusting that everyone performs their jobs and fulfills their duty efficiently. Self-respect is a significant value which enables one to realize that they have put in their best efforts.

Selfless Service

This means putting the welfare of the country and the military, as well as the unit before your own. A soldier serves a purpose larger than simply one person. It means serving the country by performing the duty loyally without expecting to gain a reward or recognition in return. Commitment to the military and to the team is the basic building block of this value.

Honor

It means living up to the values of the military. The military awards a Medal of Honor to those soldiers who make honor the biggest aspect of their life. The soldiers who are honorable in performing their duty and even their day to day tasks are appreciated and considered as strength of the country. When you leave the military, "honorable discharge" is what you want. There are other types of discharges as well, like medical discharge and what not!

Integrity

This means doing things right, morally and legally. This is a quality that one develops when they adhere to the moral principles. It means not doing or saying what may deceive or hurt others. Once the integrity of an individual starts to grow, so does the trust others put in them.

Personal Courage

This means facing adversity, danger, and fear with courage. This is a value and trait that has long been associated with military. This is difficult to master and may even mean risking your personal safety but it helps an individual stay on the right path.

If you too have the desire to join the military, here are a few things you must follow before you visit the recruiting center:

- Do your homework and read about the position you are interested in
- Take with you all of your necessary identifications, like your driver's license, birth certificate, and social security card
- Ensure you don't wear clothing with obscene images and remove all body piercings
- If you wear contacts or glasses, bring along your eyeglass case, as well as a lens container and solution
- Ensure you have a good night's sleep
- Arrive early
- Be yourself and ask that recruiter lots of questions

After meeting my recruiter, I received all the information about studying for the ASVAB (Armed Services Vocational Aptitude Battery) test, academic credentials documentations I needed to prove my education, proof of my residence in the USA, and all other required details. I found out very quickly that the ASVAB test questions had a lot to do with what you study in high school in the American education system. This became a quick challenge for me since I had attended high school, senior 1 and 2 (9th and10thgrade in the US. System),, in Uganda. Even-though the Ugandan education system is competitive, there are still a whole lot of concepts that I needed to learn very quickly. For example, I don't remember learning anything extensive about electronics and automotive at Kigezi High School. Nevertheless, I studied hard, took an ASVAB practice test, and failed it on my first try. I studied harder, took the second practice test, and passed it comfortably. Once I passed the practice test, and lined up all my other requirements, it was time to take the real ASVAB exam at the testing center recommended by my recruiter.

The process of joining the military officially completes once the candidate meets all the requirements at MEPS. This process might take two days. Let me explain all the steps that I had to go through in order for me to join the military in detail:

Step 1: Taking the ASVAB (Armed Services Vocational Aptitude Battery) Exam

This is a multiple choice test that helps determine the career which is best suited for the candidate. This test is available in both computer based and pen-paper version. This is a three-hour long exam and covers basic questions in subjects like science, writing, English, and Mathematics. There are some American schools that administer ASVAB exams, and in case you have already taken this test, then it is best to inform the center and see if your score is valid.

Step 2: Passing the Physical Examination

The physical requirements were discussed with me beforehand and this exam was a simple medical test which is

similar to that one goes through at the typical family doctors office. The different tests included:
- Muscle group and joint maneuvers,
- Drug and alcohol tests,
- Urine and blood tests,
- Hearing and vision examinations,
- Height and weight measurements,
- Specialized tests

Step 3: Meeting with the Counselor

When I cleared the ASVAB test requirements as well as the Physical examination, I was scheduled to meet with the counselor, who discussed the jobs available to me based on my score on the ASVAB test. There are different factors that contribute towards career selection, and some of them are:
- My ASVAB Score;
- My preference;
- Jobs that were available to me at that time based on the needs of the US. Army at that time.

The service enlistment counselor went over all the enlistment agreements with me. It was necessary that I fully understood the agreements before I signed on the dotted line. After the entire ordeal, I picked military policy, AKA MP -a profession in the US. Army that deals with overall law enforcement in the military. It felt like I was buying a house again ... too many pages to sign. When you sign that agreement, you are making a serious commitment with the military. You will also be required to get fingerprinted for the records as this is necessary for security clearances and background checks.

Step 4: Taking the Oath of Enlistment

Once my career within the military was determined, I was ready to take the Oath of Enlistment. In this oath, I had to vow to defend the constitution of America and to obey the UCMJ (Uniform Code of Military Justice). My family was also invited to this ceremony and watched me take this oath. Here is the oath I took:

"I, (name), do solemnly swear (or affirm) that I will support and defend the Constitution of the United States against all enemies, foreign and domestic; that I will bear true faith and allegiance to the same; and that I will obey the orders of the President of the United States and the orders of the officers appointed over me, according to regulations and the Uniform Code of Military Justice. So help me God"."

Step 5: After MEPs

As per my terms of enlistment, I had to do one of the two things mentioned below:

• Direct Ship – you will report to Basic Training between two days and two months after the MEPS testing requirement has been completed. You will be provided with instructions regarding the transportation to basic training.

• (DEP) Delayed Entry Program – you will commit to basic training at a specific time in future, typically within a year. This is usually popular among the recruits who have enlisted before their high school completion. These recruits have the option to return home till they are asked to report for duty.

When I managed to pass the ASVAB test on my first attempt things started rolling from there for me. The minute I glimpsed my score displayed on the screen, I immediately headed to the office for further discussion. If you are considering joining the US military, I recommend you study hard so that you have a high score on your ASVAB. The higher the score is, the more options you have to choose from. Based on my score and the opportunities discussed with me, I remember thinking over about which of those opportunities would help me succeed in life, while at the same time help me take care of other people. I picked becoming a military police officer. After all of the formalities were completed and I was officially sworn in, it hit me that I was now a recruit in the US military. I also came to learn about the many benefits that military service members enjoy once they become the part of the military. These include low cost travel, 30 days' paid vacations, dental and medical care, education, and much more.

In more detail, following are some military benefits the US military soldiers can avail themselves of:

Job Training

All the recruits are trained as per their job specialty. There are numerous military schools offering high tech training and most of them are also accredited. This meant that I could earn college credits while receiving my job training. An individual's determination, motivation, physical abilities, and aptitudes all assists in deciding which military career is best for them. A majority of the military jobs have their civilian counterparts, which means that military service members have a head start if they decide to leave the military.

College Money

The military wants all its soldiers to excel and thrive. During and after the service, the US military encourages its soldiers to pursue further education. For this, there are plenty of programs that can assist in paying the tuition for college. Tuition Assistance, Loan Repayment Programs,

Post-9/11 GI Bill, as well as college credit for training are some of many options available.

Promotions, Allowances and Pay

All the service members are paid two times a month on the basis of their service time, service requirements, and pay grade. A paycheck typically includes base pay as well as special allowances, and pays as per the service member's eligibility. There are numerous types of allowance granted to the service members including cost-of-living adjustments, basic allowance for subsistence, basic allowance for housing, and more.

The promotions in Military are granted on the basis of a combination of time served, job performance, and knowledge at that level, service needs, and physical fitness. The individuals who join the enlisted ranks are usually promoted thrice in their initial first four years of enlistment. The officers are promoted twice within the same period.

Free Health Care

The active members receive free dental and medical care. Wellness and care programs are available for the service members via a system of civilian and military health care facilities. Additionally, the dependent children and spouse of an active duty member can also enroll in the military health care services, though there is a small enrollment annual fee that applies.

Vacations

The military service members are eligible for 30 days paid vacation every year, as compared to the standard 2 weeks' vacation for the entry level civilian careers. Not only this, but the service members also have access to low cost and sometimes even free travel throughout the world on military aircraft.

Retirement

Certain service members make a career out of the military and these individuals are very well compensated. Once they complete 15 years of service, they have to make a decision regarding their retirement plan. The two options they have are:

• Opt for a specific amount of cash once their 15 years are completed and receive a retirement fund after 20 years which equals 40% of their highest pay.

• Opt for no cash bonus once their 15 years are completed but get the retirement fund after 20 years which equals 50% of their highest pay.

In either scenario, the individual can count on having money available to them once they retire.

Life Insurance

Life insurance is a policy that helps financially support dependent family members and friends of an individual who dies. An active duty military member is eligible for getting Service Group Life Insurance at a low monthly cost which will be deducted automatically from the monthly paycheck.

VA Benefits

The department of Veterans Affairs (VA) offers numerous federal benefits to the veterans as well as their dependents. These benefits include disability compensation, educational assistance, home loans and so much more. A military veteran can apply for a home loan that has been guaranteed by the federal government.

Thrift Saving Plan

The TSP (Thrift Saving Plan) is an investment and retirement saving plan managed by the government and is similar to the 401(k) plan. As per the discretion of the service member, a certain amount would be deducted from the pretax pay and will be invested. There won't be any taxes applied to the investment earning till you start withdrawing the cash once you retire.

More Lifestyle Benefits

There are numerous companies that offer special discounts and deals to former and current service members as a way for thanking and supporting them for their services.

You may be wondering what type of basic training I had to go through once I enlisted in the military. The basic training, also known as IET (Initial Entry Training) and informally known as Boot Camp, is a training of mental and physical fitness to prepare the recruit to become an efficient soldier of the US military. This training is carried out in numerous different posts around the US. This training is designed to be extremely challenging and intense. The challenge not only comes from the complex and severe physical training but also from the psychological adjustments to the unusual way of living.

The basic training has two major categories – Basic Combat Training and Advanced Individual Training. Both these training programs help the recruits in preparing for all the required service elements – emotional, mental, and physical. It provides the new soldiers the basic tools needed to execute their tasks that will be expected from them during a mission. Whichever service you opt for, be it Army, Air Force, Navy, Coastal Guard, or Marine Corps, they have their own training program that is tailored according to the specialized nature of their role in the US military. Whichever branch of service you have selected, the basic training will be a challenging and intense experience.

Roughly 90% of recruits are able to successfully complete their initial 6 months of service. The main aim of these training programs isn't to 'break' recruits as commonly assumed by the masses. In fact, the mixture of classroom time, field exercises, and physical training helps the recruits in getting more capable and stronger. It is indeed a tough process, but it is also a rewarding one that you are bound to value throughout your life.

CHAPTER 9

Reaping Rewards and Giving Back

I could feel myself quickly dying. Peering up from the bottom of the deep end of the pool, through the shimmering surface, I could see the shape of my wife sitting at the waters' edge. My two sons who had been splashing around behind me just a few minutes ago were now out of view. Sunk like a rock on the floor, I could no longer hold my breath and a sensation of life slipping away enveloped me.

Suddenly, panic and disorientation set in. I raised my hands in an effort to both surface and signal for help. Why wasn't my wife coming to my aid? Could she not see I was drowning? Then I blacked out.

I was at the edge of the pool. The muffled sound of kids screaming slowly filtered into full volume. Beside me, my wife was panting heavily on all fours while screaming at me for almost drowning her as well. I could barely move but was involuntarily coughing out liquid. Sounds slowly started to crystallize and my vision was beginning to come back. I sucked in several breaths of fresh air as I looked around shakily, amazed and grateful to be alive. My wife, with one arm locked in position from a recent car accident, had just saved my life. We lay together recovering our breath while our boys looked on.

The day had began innocuously enough. A colleague of mine at work had invited my family and I over for a summer barbecue get-together. I packed up a small DJ rig and we headed out for a day of fun and friendship. Once we arrived I set up my system to play music in a loop and then joined everyone in the festivities. After eating, a small group of people jumped into the pool and began swimming and splashing while the rest settled around the property huddling in conversation. My two sons were in the pool while my wife relaxed in the gazebo nearby.

The water looked cool and inviting on that sweltering day. I didn't know how to swim, but figured I could get myself into the pool and pull myself along the edge using the handrails. My shorts and under-armor shirt would be fine to swim with, so I jumped into the shallow end and starting pulling myself along. Making it all the way around the pool, I decided to go again. At that moment, my wife came down from the gazebo and pulled up a chair at the pool's edge. We smiled at each other as I pulled myself along towards the deep end. When I got to the corner, I pushed off the side and reached for the other rail. Mistiming my reach, I grabbed for the rail early and plunged into the water.

I tumbled towards the bottom, losing orientation for which way was up or down. Techniques for how to save myself failed to materialize in my mind. I raised my arms towards the surface, hoping somebody would see me and rescue me from my demise. My gaze fixed upon my wife's shadow, then all went dark.

That incident and many others gave me an appreciation for life and my good fortune in ways I cannot explain in words. After many years living in America, I was reaping the rewards of fortune and hard work. I had been a good husband and father, persevered as a law-abiding citizen, and given back to the country by, among other things, joining the army. Now I had been saved from certain drowning and I felt very blessed.

Through numerous struggles and many ups and downs, you will find yourself eventually in a position to take stock of your life. If all goes well, you too will eventually reap the rewards of the good fortune of living in the United States, and when you do, find ways to give back in your own way. Here are some thoughts I have that I would like you to consider:

This Chapter's Takeaways

By nature, I truly believe that everyone on this planet is blessed no matter what we think. Throughout the world, the word blessing is used countless times. God is the one who gives blessings. As for me, I strongly go by Psalm 71:6 – "From birth I have relied on you; you brought me forth from my mother's womb. I will ever praise you."

I also believe in Acts 17:26, "From one man he made every nation of men that they should inhibit the whole earth; and he determined the times set for them and the exact places where they should live."

Among so many great verses in the bible, I thank God that he blessed me with all that I am and have, be it possessions, family, friends, the promised eternal life, when he placed me on this planet.

I believe that the very basic factor of living a blessed life is to know yourself first. It may sound simple, but in reality is a challenging thing to do. To properly understand yourself, you need focused introspection, which is difficult to do since a majority of us have created layers of denial about ourselves. I suggest conducting an honest assessment about how you can help yourself. Start by exploring your deepest desires, passions, and fears, things that make you insecure, proud, happy, sad, and excited. You need to realize how blessed you are once you honestly try to understand yourself. You will start appreciating God and His blessings upon you. If you don't understand yourself or appreciate the skills and abilities God has given you, how can you expect others to appreciate you, and how will you appreciate the countless other blessings God has given you? This is the reason I believe that living a blessed and happy life starts with ourselves.

You must determine what a beautiful life means to you. It is essential for us to understand that material things aren't what make up a beautiful life. For me, my wife, my sons, my family, my friends, my colleagues, my struggles, my achievements, and so many more blessings are what make up my beautiful life. Ask yourself what is missing in your life. Is it love? Inspiration? Happiness? Is there too much negativity in your life? Are there people who discourage you or don't support you? Are you your own problem? Do you think you don't deserve a blessed life? Do you need to change your perception about yourself and about life in general?

Staying positive, being thankful to God for all the blessings He bestowed upon you, removing negative thoughts and negative people; all this can lead you towards a happy life. You need to start working towards living a beautiful and blessed life. Everyone has their fair share of struggles, pressures, and problems. I did too, but this didn't mean I stopped appreciating life. Those hurdles and problems actually helped me in appreciating my life more. I realized who truly loved and cared about me. I realized how blessed I was to have such a supportive family, such strong father figures, and such amazing friends, and I also realized how all the tough training and other challenging experiences during my time in the military helped shape my life for the better.

I learned that it is essential to eliminate the unnecessary and negative things from your life and focus on the positive aspects to be truly happy in life. I learned the importance of taking time off to have some quality 'me' time, and the value of making memories with my loved ones. Such moments really help one appreciate all that God has granted us and helps us learn to be more thankful for all the blessings.

I know a lot of you are living a truly blessed and beautiful life already and are thankful for your blessings. However, there might be many of you who are struggling. To you, I want to say, "Don't lose hope, the best is yet to come."

Here are a few strategies that I rely on that can also help you in appreciating your blessings and living a happier life:

Surround Yourself with Loved Ones

To enjoy a happy and blessed life, we must be surrounded by positive individuals who truly love and care about us. I learned to stay away from scornful and negative people. You must have a closer association with caring and positive people who have a good influence on your life.

Resort to Fairness

A noble and good heart is essential for a blessed life. We must let go of anger, jealousy, and bitterness. God bestows His blessings on everyone during different stages of our life. We must deal with everyone and everything with patience, kindness, and love.

Be More Generous

We must share our blessings with others who are in need and God shall grant us even more.

Be Hardworking

In order to live a happy life, we must focus on maintaining efficiency and infusing a high level of quality to whatever we do. God blesses the ones who are diligent in what they do.

Live in Unity

God has asked us all to live in harmony and unity. When people are united, there are fewer arguments and selfish skirmishes that generally lead to increased negativity in our lives.

Appreciate Your Life

Creating a beautiful life is not an easy task. There are bound to be challenges and hurdles in your way, but you must focus on everything positive in your life to help you face all your problems. Allow yourself to feel good about you and your surroundings. Begin appreciating even the little things that make you happy.

Lower Your Expectations

This is one of the most important lessons I have learned in my life. High expectations are the root cause of disappointments. This is a mistake which a majority of us make. We start having high expectations from ourselves, our family, our friends, and from everything in general. This is what leads to sadness and even depression. So, it is better not to have unrealistic and high expectations from anyone, even ourselves.

Respect Others

This is something that my dear mother taught me and I strongly live by. I also teach my sons to always be respectful towards others no matter what happens. I believe this is a crucial value which everyone should uphold as a core value.

Be Calm

You can avoid so many unnecessary problems, stress, and negativity simply if you keep calm in all situations that come your way. It can also help you in remembering to count your blessings, especially when you are down.

These are a few principles I live by and which I believe have played a significant role in leading me towards the blessed life I am living. If you keep remembering to count your blessings, you will realize what a wonderful life you are living and you will come to this realization as well that life is indeed beautiful and is a wonderful blessing from God.

CHAPTER 10

Living the Dream

I set out toward a section of a wooded area in my village of Kyobugombe to chop some firewood, then headed to a shallow brook to wash up and fetch water. By now, my sister and other relatives were returning home from digging in the farm, and I trailed behind them, my skinny frame straining at the load. I carried the plastic jerry can of water and sack of firewood a mile to my mother's home. One of my aunts had prepared supper and all relatives in the area were invited. Some of my favorite foods had been prepared; matooke (bananas prepared while the skin is still green), fresh beans, cabbage, groundnut paste, and emondi (potatoes). I raced over and wedged myself in between a couple of my cousins lined up against the mud wall. We snaked forward, and when it was my turn, I piled as much food on the small plate as would fit, then sat on the floor and delighted in my time eating as the elders regaled us with tales of the past.

After the meal, a group of friends gathered in a nearby grassy clearing for a game of soccer using a ball fashioned from banana fibers. We picked sides and played barefoot until the daylight started to fade, then congratulated ourselves and dispersed to our homes for the night. As I lay on the floor mat in the room illuminated by the dim light from a paraffin lantern, swatting away mosquitoes and listening to the howl of stray dogs in the distance, I tried to envision how I could direct my future. The thought of growing up here in this state of extreme poverty made me feel sad. For any chance of a brighter future, I was going to have to get out of this village and move someplace else. But how was I going to accomplish this? I had no answers, but before I fell asleep, I said a silent prayer for God to deliver a path for me to move to America.

A few months later I was sitting at my desk at Kigezi High School when the principal entered our classroom and called out a name. The name he called was mine, but I didn't acknowledge hearing it and kept my head down in fear. Usually if the principal demanded to see you, it meant you were in trouble of some sort. He called my name again, and this time the teacher looked in my direction and motioned for me to come forward. I pushed off from the wooden desk and crept forward. The principal was already plodding back toward the main office so I ran to catch up. When I entered his office, I was startled to see my sister standing there.

"Take it easy, Dixion, you're not in trouble," he grinned, noticing the rigidity in my frame.

"You've been summoned by your uncle," he announced. "He wants you to meet him in Kabale town. He has some news about your petition to move to the United States."

I gulped and glanced over at my sister. She looked as nervous as I felt.

"He wants to see us right now?" I stammered.

"Yes, he sent someone to pick you up. You can leave right away."

My sister grabbed my hand, and we dashed out of the office into the parking lot. I recognized a family friend waving at us and we headed toward the waiting taxi. Burning with anticipation, we hopped into the taxi and started the ride from school to the town of Kabale to meet with my uncle. The trip was a short distance to travel, but minutes seemed like hours and yards felt like miles. Our first endeavor at obtaining a visa to go to the United States had concluded in failure. Since then, I had no knowledge about another attempt, and had no inkling what the result of this undertaking could have been. My sister and I worked in vain to extract information from our family friend. She had nothing to reveal so we quit begging and chatted about other matters of interest.

We arrived in Kabale and made our way through the small town toward my uncle's residence. Upon arrival we drove into the courtyard and rode past the "boy's quarters" to the main house. My sister beat me to the front door and rapped on it hard. Initially cautious, one of the house cleaners opened the door slightly; then recognized us and smiled as she opened it fully. We rushed in, and through the entrance saw my uncle seated in the living room. As a town council member he regularly dressed in suit and tie, even while at home. Upon hearing us come in, he got up and flashed a warm smile in our direction.

"Are you prepared to move abroad?" he beamed, taking enormous satisfaction in possessing information powerful enough to arrest us dead in our tracks. He didn't have to tell us where we were going. Only one place warranted this level of drama.

"Stop kidding!" my sister squealed, as I stood next to her in shock and disbelief.

"I'm not joking. Your petition was approved," he declared.

The words reverberated like music and lingered in the air like the aromatic scent of local bougainvillea blossoms. I should have been elated, but now my mind raced with a million questions. I would be leaving behind all that I knew for a country where everything would be different. Would I be capable of adapting and conforming? Would this "new world" turn out to be all that I dreamed? Would I make everyone who toiled hard on this petition proud? I had seldom left my hometown of Kabale, and soon I would be living thousands of miles away in an unfamiliar country surrounded by a few family members and many strangers. Coming from a village where most people knew each other, this was hard to envision.

After several moments in a trance, I jerked back into the moment and felt exhilaration and joy surge through my body. This is what I had been praying for all this time. I knew that my uncle wouldn't play a cruel joke on us, but demanded to see evidence of approval in order to accept this was taking place. I asked him if there was any paperwork and he presented me my new passport with a permanent visa stamped on one of the pages. My eyes widened as I let out a small yelp. He stated proudly that our appeal had been won, and as a result the denial had been overturned. I was thankful and began pondering all the opportunities I would have once I arrived in America and how I would make my mother proud.

My nervousness turned suddenly into excitement, and I was now bursting to relieve myself. My uncle pointed me to a bathroom, and I dashed in, slamming the door behind. I expected to see a hole in the floor like I was used to in the village, but instead found myself face-to-face with an apparatus I had no idea how to use. I stared at it for a few moments. It appeared to me like a puzzle that needed solving. Looking down into the water, I couldn't figure out how to position myself in order to take care of business. I imagined that perhaps I should squat on it. After some thought, it occurred to me that I could use it by simply standing close to the base and aiming down or sitting on the round seat. I sat down and let loose. In under a minute I had carried out the critical task, but then was perplexed about what to do next. The waste wasn't going anywhere on its own, and since I hadn't observed any in there when I came in, couldn't imagine I should leave mine. I hit upon a solution that involved a lot of mess and not much finesse. The scene was not pretty.

Once I was done I inquired if there was a different washroom I could use. My uncle informed me they had a pit latrine in the back yard, and I told him I would be taking advantage of that one for the remainder of the time I was staying. He chuckled and said he understood. Apparently, they received many visitors from the village who were equally bewildered about how to use a flushable toilet as I was. Chin dipped down and arms tucked in at my sides, I grinned sheepishly and sprinted out to clean up for the day's activities.

My uncle offered to accompany my sister and I to a clinic in Kampala to begin our medical checkups required for admission into the United States. The following week we drove down. This was my second time in the capital city of the country, yet still I was awestruck at everything around me. Over the next few days, we stopped in numerous clinics around town for a myriad of checkups. During those visits, I bent and coughed, and got poked for fluids and probed for every ailment imaginable. In between visits to the clinics, we shopped around for clothing that we would require for the frigid February weather in Maryland. We went from building to building, obtaining signatures for multiple official documents. At the American consulate in Kampala, an official handed us a thick, sealed package.

"These are NOT to be opened until you get to the emigration office at Dulles Airport," he warned.

We replied that we understood and kept the package sealed. More days went by, and after three weeks of sweating our way up and down the hills of Kampala in the equatorial heat, we finally completed the checklist of requirements necessary to enter the United States. All that remained was to convey our final goodbyes to everyone we knew and head to the airport to start on our journey pursuing the American dream.

This Chapter's Takeaways

I eventually arrived in the United States, and a couple of decades later I finally feel I've accomplished my vision of the American Dream. What is the American Dream, you may ask?

Living the American Dream is what we make it to be. I now live in a country with beautiful seasons (Fall being my favorite), beautiful people, and lots of opportunities. Each country on this planet has its advantages and drawbacks. I happen to have been blessed to live in two beautiful countries that I believe were perfect for me.

In America, the American Dream is a term everyone around the globe is familiar with, first used in the book "The Epic of America" by James Truslow Adams. During this time, America was suffering from the Great Depression. The American Dream was utilized by Adams to explain the social and political expectations, religious promises, and complex beliefs. This term has since become widespread and describes the American way of life.

There isn't a right definition or explanation of this term. The American Dream represents individuality and freedom of living the way one wants to. Many historians state that The American Dream begins its roots during the Declaration of Independence with an idea that each man and woman, irrespective of their birth, will achieve what they are able to. Each individual will be seen and treated equally and will be recognized by others for what they have achieved. In order to make this dream come true, all Americans have to work together. The American Dream is for every American, irrespective of their social, racial or religious affiliation.

According to Adams, there have been many Americans who mistrust this 'American Dream' because they weren't able to achieve what they wanted or hoped for. For many individuals, this dream is associated with becoming rich and achieving anything if they work hard for it. However, for many others this dream goes way beyond materialism, as for them it is more about living a happy, content, and fulfilling life. For many, this dream is about liberty and opportunity.

The American Dream has had different meanings throughout the history of America. Today, this dream refers to the idea that one's success is dependent upon their hard work and abilities, rather than their class structure. Some believe they have a better chance of achieving success and prosperity in America than they could achieve in their own country, while others also believe that there is an opportunity for their children to get an excellent education and enjoy great career opportunities. For some, it is about embracing their individuality without any constraints that have been imposed by ethnicity, gender, race, caste, or class.

The definition of American Dream has constantly been under debate and discussion. However, the general idea is associated with actions, assumptions, and beliefs of individual freedom, equality, and pursuit of your dreams. The American Dream has captured the imagination of individuals from around the country, from all walks of life. It has attracted millions of people towards America in the hopes of living this American Dream. Its essence could be found throughout the history and culture of America – in the soaring oratory of Martin Luther, in the poetry of Carl Sandburg, in the music of Aaron Copland, in the hopes of a single mother, in the belief of a struggling teenager, and throughout the sacrifices and efforts of the first generation of Americans to provide a better future for their children.

I believe that the American Dream constitutes of three main elements.

The first element is about the freedom of pursuing one's passions and interests in life. In order to do so, it is important for us to strive towards our true potential. Even though the specific interests and passions that people pursue are wide ranging and varied, the liberty of engaging in those pursuits is seen as paramount. The capability of doing so allows people to develop their talents and start living out their dreams. America is a country that encourages and allows this to happen. This country has made it possible for me to aim high and achieve my dreams and passions. It has given me the freedom and courage to dream and given me the opportunity to pursue them.

The second element of the American Dream is the economic well-being and security. This means having the tools and resources of living a rewarding and comfortable life. This includes having a decent job, providing for your children's future, owning a home, saving up, and retiring in comfort. These are rewards one gets for following the rules and working hard. I am fortunate enough to enjoy these rewards. I have a good job, enough to provide for the needs of my family, and my kids are getting a good education. My hard work and determination has led to economic and financial security in my life and for my family's life.

The third element of the American Dream is the significance of having optimism and hope with respect to witnessing progress in one's life. It is all about confidently moving forward and facing the challenges that lie ahead while having a strong belief that you can overcome those challenges. I believe that Americans are an optimistic group of people and the American Dream directly reflects this optimism. I have observed a strong belief held by most Americans that the best days are ahead of us. This optimism and hope in the progress doesn't merely apply to our own life but to the lives of our children and the generations to come ... the future of this wonderful country as a whole.

These three basic elements, I believe, are what constitute the foundation of American Dream. These are the essential components of what living a good life looks like in America. They remind us about the struggles and sacrifices made by the individuals who came before us as well as our own. It reminds us about the blessings that come in to our lives due to our hard work and determination. It reminds us about what this country has given us all and how truly blessed we are to become a living testimony to be part of the American Dream.

What does it truly mean to me to be living the dream? I personally believe that I have been blessed, starting from my home village in Uganda, to my new home town in America. I have been blessed with a great mother, who instilled in me the values that I live by today. I have been blessed to have the right kind of guidance from my father figures. I thank grandpa and Uncle Kabuchu. I know I am blessed to have the most beautiful Flower as my wife, and the most handsome, well-behaved sons as my family. I am blessed because I have other relatives that love me unconditionally. I am blessed because God has put great friends in my life who I count on every day for guidance and comradery. I am blessed because I am alive and writing this book. I thank God for this very moment as my fingers finish typing these statements. And I sincerely hope that you too will achieve your goal of living the American Dream.

A WORD OF THANKS

I thank God for the wisdom He bestowed upon me and for allowing me to live my dream. Jesus, you are my savior, you are my strength, and my guidance. Praise be to God Almighty!

I want to thank my wife and children for bearing with me during the entire duration of writing this book, and for always supporting and encouraging me to move on and follow my dreams. My Flower, thanks for putting up with my mid-night inspirations of writing yet another anecdote for this book.

In addition, I want to thank my editor and the proof readers for their crucial support and feedback that helped me shape the story of my life into a book.

Finally, I want to thank you, the reader, for taking time to read this book, and I hope you learned something from it. If you feel inspired, please recommend this book to another reader and leave a review on any platform of your choice (e.g. Amazon, etc.), or send your valuable feedback and comments to me at drdeilbooks@gmail.com.

Thanks again for reading my book, and May God bless you!

You Too Can Live The Dream.

A young Dixion Rwakasyaguri (LEFT) in Kyobugombe, Uganda.

Dixion Rwakasyaguri in America as night shift Nursing Assistant.

Dixion Rwakasyaguri taking his studies seriously. Keys to success.

Dixion Rwakasyaguri and his "Flower".

Dixion Rwakasyaguri and his "Flower". Early dating days.

Beaming bride and groom. Wedding bells.

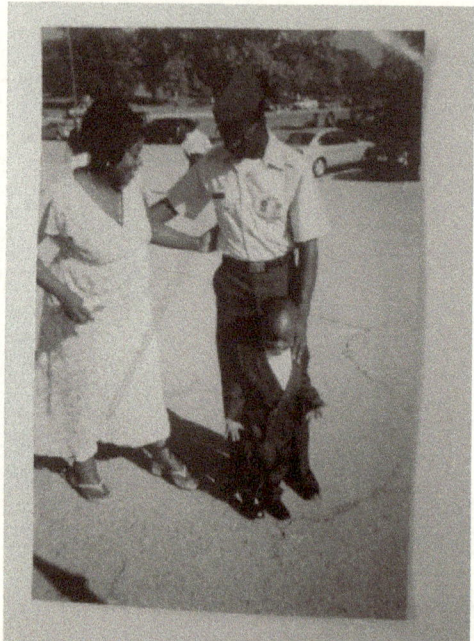
Dixion Rwakasyaguri. Graduation day from boot camp.

Dixion Rwakasyaguri. Preparing for deployment.

Dixion Rwakasyaguri.

Dixion Rwakasyaguri.

Dixion Rwakasyaguri.

Dixion Rwakasyaguri. Power nap. Weapons ready at all times.

Dixion Rwakasyaguri. Meal time on base. Staying fit and healthy.

Dixion Rwakasyaguri. On base. Out for some fresh air.

Dixion Rwakasyaguri. Preparing to deploy on another long mission.

Dixion Rwakasyaguri in his driveway. No mowing the lawn today.

Dixion Rwakasyaguri at work. All that studying paid off.

Dixion Rwakasyaguri braving ocean with sons after surviving drowning.

You Too Can Live The Dream | 139

Dixion Rwakasyaguri handling barbecue in backyard of his dream home.

Dixion Rwakasyaguri in the driveway of his dream home.

Dixion Rwakasyaguri and his wife in the driveway of their dream home.

Dixion Rwakasyaguri and his sons in the driveway of their dream home.

Dixion Rwakasyaguri and his wife in their driveway.

Dixion Rwakasyaguri. Family photo. Smile! You're Living the Dream.

www.ingramcontent.com/pod-product-compliance
Lightning Source LLC
Chambersburg PA
CBHW032124090426
42743CB00007B/450